Forfeiting Our Property Rights

Forfeiting Our Property Rights

Is *Your* Property Safe from Seizure?

Rep. Henry Hyde

CATO INSTITUTE

Washington, D.C.

Library of Congress Cataloging-in-Publication Data

Hyde. Henry J.
  Forfeiting our property rights : is your property safe from
seizure? / Rep. Henry Hyde.
      p.   cm.
  Includes bibliographical references and index.
  ISBN 1-882577-18-3. — ISBN 1-882577-19-1 (pbk.)
    1. Forfeiture—United States.   2. Searches and seizures—United
States.   3. Right of property—United States.   I. Title.
KF9747.H93   1995
345.73′.0522—dc20
[347.305522]   95-10701
                                                                             CIP

"Presumed Guilty" by Andrew Schneider and Mary Pat Flaherty was
originally published in the *Pittsburgh Press*. Used by permission of the
Pittsburgh Post-Gazette.

Cover Design by Colin Moore.

Printed in the United States of America.

CATO INSTITUTE
1000 Massachusetts Ave., N.W.
Washington, D.C. 20001

Contents

Foreword

The stories in this book will make your blood boil. Is this America at the close of the 20th century? If it seems more like medieval Europe, when lords held all but unaccountable power over their subjects, it is because that is the origin of modern American forfeiture law. Revived and driven by the war on drugs, that law today is being used across this nation to make a mockery of our rights to property and due process and is now reaching well beyond the war on drugs. It is to the credit of Henry Hyde—no pandering liberal he—that a spotlight is shining at last on this dark corner of our law.

What are we to say when officers in the Sheriff's Department in Volusia County, Florida, stop thousands of motorists traveling Interstate 95 who fit a "drug-courier profile," then simply confiscate, on the spot, any funds those motorists are carrying in excess of $100; when a Minneapolis man convicted of selling seven "obscene" magazines and videotapes is fined $100,000, given a sentence of six years, and then made to forfeit 10 pieces of commercial real estate, 31 current or former businesses, including all of their assets, and nearly $9 million; when police drain the bank account of a Bakersfield, California, woman after her son, who had not lived with her for 10 years, is arrested on drug trafficking charges; or when 30 local, state, and federal agents burst into a Malibu, California, home—nominally in a fruitless search for drugs, but actually, as a subsequent investigation brings out, as part of a forfeiture action—during the course of which they shoot and kill the owner?

Those examples of modern forfeiture law in practice are not made up. What is worse, they are a tiny sample of the kinds of abuses of government power we find everywhere today under this body of law, which encourages and even sanctions practices we would never tolerate in other areas of our law. If he had done nothing else, then, Congressman Hyde would deserve our thanks for having drawn together in one place so wide a variety of such cases, to give life to the problem before us and hope to the victims of this runaway law.

But he has done much more in this book. Among other things, Mr. Hyde helps us to see just how we got into this mess, through an accumulation of "hoary doctrines" resurrected from the past, only to be given judicial and statutory sanction over the years. And he helps us too to see our way out, with his own proposed bill to bring much-needed reform to this law.

Finding its roots in the Old Testament—in the idea that objects and animals could be "guilty" of wrongdoing; in medieval doctrine—in the forfeiture of such "deodands" to the Crown; and in admiralty law—in the seizure of ships and cargo for failure to pay customs duties, forfeiture has been with us since our inception as a nation. With the war on drugs, however, it has taken on a life of its own.

Although modern asset forfeiture law varies by federal or state statute, the essence of the law is simple and stark. Stated operationally, under most civil asset forfeiture statutes, as opposed to criminal statutes, law enforcement officials can seize a person's property, real or chattel, without notice or hearing, upon an *ex parte* showing of mere probable cause to believe that the property has somehow been involved in a crime. Proceeding thus *in rem*—against the property, not the person—the government need not charge the owner or anyone else with a crime, for the action is against "the property." The allegation of "involvement" may range from a belief that the property is contraband to a belief that it represents the proceeds of crime (even if the property is in the hands of someone not suspected of a crime), that it is an instrumentality of crime, or that it somehow "facilitates" crime. And the showing of probable cause may be based on nothing more than hearsay, innuendo, or even the paid, self-serving testimony of a party with interests adverse to the owner.

Once the property is seized, the burden is upon the owner, if he wants to try to get his property back, to prove its "innocence," not by a probable-cause but by a preponderance-of-the-evidence standard. Until recently, that proof has been all but impossible because the thing is considered to be the offender. Imbued with personality, the thing is said to be "tainted" by its unlawful use. Thus, the rights of the owner never come into consideration. Given the manifest injustice in that, Congress and several states in the 1980s enacted innocent-owner defenses. But under those defenses the owner must prove that he

viii

lacked both control over the property's unlawful use and knowledge of the use—negatives that are often impossible to prove. Moreover, before the Supreme Court reined in the "relation-back" doctrine in 1993—which holds that title to property vests in the government at the time it is used illegally, even if the property changes hands many times after that—those few owners who could prove their innocence often lost because the relation-back doctrine was said to trump the innocent-owner defense.

The substantive and procedural hurdles owners face are only compounded by the practical hurdles. Deprived of their property, ranging from homes, cars, boats, and airplanes to businesses and bank accounts, owners are at a distinct legal and practical disadvantage if they want to wage a costly legal battle against the government to recover the property. Moreover, if the owner has been involved in activity that in any way might lead to criminal charges—however trivial or baseless those charges might ultimately prove to be—the risk of self-incrimination entailed by any effort to get the property back has to be weighed against the value of the property, which means that the owner will often simply not make the effort.

In contrast with the civil forfeiture law just outlined, criminal forfeiture is a recent development in American law, stemming from the enactment by Congress in 1970 of the Racketeer Influenced and Corrupt Organizations Act (RICO). Although Congress has steadily increased its reach—and the RICO statute itself is extraordinarily vague—criminal forfeiture is relatively less objectionable than civil forfeiture because it is justified as punishment for a crime and thus follows only after an *in personam* proceeding against the person, not an *in rem* proceeding against the property. Defendants are thus entitled to the procedural protections of the criminal law, including the requisite burdens and standards of proof. And forfeiture turns on conviction, not on the antiquated fictions of civil forfeiture. Although criminal forfeiture is in a sense broader than civil forfeiture in that under it the government can reach even "untainted" assets, that result follows simply from the different rationales for criminal and civil forfeiture. Under criminal forfeiture, property is forfeited because of the guilt of the owner, not the "guilt" of the property.

Clearly, there is much that is wrong in this law, and much in it that helps to explain just why the abuses Mr. Hyde so richly documents have come about. The reader will find in this book not only an account of those wrongs but an explanation of how they lead to the abuses. Whether the remedy Mr. Hyde proposes goes far enough—whether his preservation of the "facilitation" doctrine, for example, can be justified—must be left to the reader to decide. At the least, now that Mr. Hyde is chairman of the House Judiciary Committee, there is hope for relief. This book should help to create the climate of public opinion that will be necessary to bring about that relief.

ROGER PILON

Acknowledgments

I wish to express my appreciation to the officers and staff of the Cato Institute—William A. Niskanen, chairman; Edward H. Crane, president; David Boaz, executive vice president; and Roger Pilon, director of the Center for Constitutional Studies—for their assistance and cooperation, which made this publication possible. The Cato Institute has consistently provided a much-needed and very certain trumpet among the unreasoning cacophony that is everyday Washington.

I also want to thank, for his unflagging inspiration and example, George M. Fishman, Esq., who serves as my legislative counsel in the House of Representatives, most especially for reading (in his free time) this manuscript and for making valuable suggestions (also in his free time). I owe a special debt of gratitude to Brenda Grantland, a stalwart leader in the battle for forfeiture reform; to Terrance A. Reed, whose outstanding prior legal work on forfeiture paved the way; to Robert E. Bauman, who provided invaluable assistance to me in researching the book; and to the many others who gave advice and counsel, including Nadine Strossen, president of the American Civil Liberties Union, and Nancy Hollander, president of the National Association of Criminal Defense Lawyers.

For permission to quote from the excellent forfeiture series published by each of these newspapers (and for the reporters who did the hard work), I hereby thank the *Pittsburgh Post-Gazette*, the *Orlando Sentinel*, and the *San Jose Mercury News*. A special word of appreciation to Ellen Callas and the *Financial Privacy Report* of Lafayette, California, publishers, and to the author for permission to quote from Brenda Grantland's book, *Your House Is Under Arrest: How Police Can Seize Your Home, Car, and Business Without a Trial—And How to Protect Yourself.*

I also want to thank Robert Kephart, whose militant interest in preserving individual freedom against government encroachment was in large part the inspiration for this book; and also Andrea Millen Rich, president of Laissez-Faire Books and the Center for Independent Thought, for her generous support as well.

Introduction

Impelled by the exigencies of the so-called war on drugs, the broadly written Racketeer Influenced and Corrupt Organizations Act (RICO),[1] and subsequent amendments to federal anti-drug laws, the hoary doctrines of Anglo-American civil asset forfeiture law have been resurrected, like some jurisprudential Frankenstein monster, from the dark recesses of past centuries. (If that sounds alarmingly scary, it is meant to be.) And like Mary Shelley's well-meaning fictional doctor who gave life to the mindless monster, eager federal and state legislators, and their often unquestioning judicial accomplices, seem loath to recognize the extent of the consequent destruction of our constitutional rights and basic liberties.

For the last quarter century, government's wholesale confiscation of businesses, luxury homes, jet planes, yachts, expensive autos, and millions of dollars in money-laundering bank accounts has appealed to both the American public's well-founded fear of the drug scourge and the law enforcement lobby's need for self-justifying, telegenic battle trophies. Operating in intense, symbiotic harmony with this revival of the English sovereign's arcane forfeiture powers has been the politicians' individual and collective need for easy answers to complex problems—to provide the obligatory appearance of "doing something."

As much as any citizen or any public official, I too want to rid our nation of the multifarious problems caused by drug abuse. The best ways and means to achieve that worthy goal can and should continue as a subject of rational, good-faith debate. But in my view, a drug "war" has been perverted too often into a series of frontal attacks on basic American constitutional guarantees—including due process, the presumption of innocence, and the right to own and enjoy private property. Foremost among the invasions we now witness are unrelenting government assaults on property rights, fueled by a dangerous and emotional vigilante mentality that sanctions shredding the U.S. Constitution into meaningless confetti.

1

I believe most Americans do not realize the grave extent to which our constitutional protections have been violated and diminished in recent years.

Much of what you may have learned in school or college about your rights and liberties no longer applies. Increased government and police powers, rising criminal activity and violence, popular anxiety about drug use—all have become justifications for curtailing the application of the Bill of Rights and the individual security it once guaranteed. Federal and state officials now have the power to seize your business, home, bank account, records, and personal property, all without indictment, hearing, or trial. Everything you have can be taken away at the whim of one or two federal or state officials operating in secret. Regardless of sex, age, race, or economic station, we are all potential victims. And unless these trends are recognized and reversed, there will soon be very little that individuals can do to protect their property or themselves.

I want to make clear at the outset, as a legislator and an attorney, that I do not oppose appropriate use of asset forfeiture as a means of punishing criminal acts. Criminal asset forfeiture—following a criminal conviction—is a just adjunct punishment of the guilty who have been accorded due process and a fair judicial determination of their status. Civil asset forfeiture also has its limited place in the historical context of admiralty law and the nonpayment of customs duties, both of which date from the earliest days of our nationhood. Civil forfeiture even has a proper place in the prosecution of the war on drugs, but not as it is now being abused on a wholesale basis, as you will see.

There is hope, however. A few years ago, those reading court report advance sheets began noticing a nascent trend: federal judges inveighing against the utter lack of due process in civil forfeiture proceedings.[2] And those keeping up with investigative journalism noticed a slew of newspaper and television exposés of innocent property owners being stripped of their homes, belongings, and even life itself, by overzealous law enforcement officials in hot pursuit of funds for their departmental budgets.

Major television network news programs and courageous newspapers, among them the *Pittsburgh Post-Gazette*, the *San Jose Mercury News*, and the *Orlando Sentinel*, have devoted much time and space to revelations about asset forfeiture and its impact on individual Americans.[3] As a result, the public is finally becoming aware that forfeiture laws are not only being abused by prosecutors and law enforcement officials but are being employed for ends unrelated to drug control and for dubious political or social objectives that most Americans, once given the facts, do not support. As the individual horror stories multiply, people are realizing they could easily be the next victims of government run amok.

Coincidentally, after nearly three decades of generally supine acquiescence on this issue, some state and federal judges[4] and, in 1993, a majority of the U.S. Supreme Court[5] have begun to act against the worst abuses of the forfeiture laws—albeit, some would say, only in marginal ways. Predictably, police and prosecutors have responded with dire predictions of impending disaster if asset forfeiture powers are further weakened, calling this one of their most potent weapons in the anti-drug battle—a bald assertion, questionable in itself.

Before going further, I think it appropriate to consider the basic principle that unchecked forfeiture undermines—the right to private property—and why that principle is so important in America, or in any just society. True, we are dealing with an abstract principle we usually take for granted, but the right to own and enjoy property protects and enhances the lives of all citizens. Without it, human beings are reduced to misery and want. The stark reality of this truth is never so evident as when a squad of government agents breaks down your door, guns drawn, and confiscates your family home. That may sound dramatic. But too often that is the reality of modern American forfeiture law.

The right to ownership of property is implicit in the Seventh Commandment, "Thou shalt not steal." Those who distinguish between property rights and "human rights" commit a fundamental error—property rights are human rights, among the most important of all human rights. To exist and prosper, every human being needs material goods—property. A person cannot live without the means to support life. We all have the right to supply our needs by using what we own—our "Lives, Liberties, and Estates," as John Locke put it—free from disturbance by others. I believe, as did St. Thomas Aquinas, and Aristotle before him,[6] that the natural law recognizes in every person this right to property.

Through the ages we have devised an equitable, peaceable, and effective system to satisfy human needs. In Western civilization we call this system "private ownership" of property. It is an orderly structure that avoids the sure chaos of common control, permitting the individual to sustain life and grow. No better proof of this can be found than in the abject failure of those systems that have forbidden the ownership of private property, such as communism, or seriously curtailed its enjoyment, such as socialism.

I also think it evident that an individual's free nature indicates clearly that we are self-providers, that we naturally want to support ourselves and our families. But when an individual is robbed of his or her property, of the right to ownership of material goods, that individual then becomes subject to the will, caprice, and power of others in a way that degrades the dignity and independence of his or her human nature. And when this power is concentrated in the hands of government, it becomes an even greater threat to life and liberty.

In a free society, then, individuals provide for their needs by exercising the right of ownership for themselves and their families. The right to own and use property enhances our relations with other individuals and the well-being of our families and promotes peace and stability in the general community. Based on centuries of experience, we as a nation have come to understand that private ownership of property, tempered by appropriate social control, is the only practicable system. The pages of the Constitution and the Bill of Rights confirm this view repeatedly.

That is why the unfettered use of civil forfeiture strikes at the very heart of the American and Judeo-Christian experience. It violates not only constitutional and political rights but the principles of nature designed to protect and preserve all mankind. Cast in that light, the forfeiture issue acquires a much different and far more sinister meaning for each of us.

My personal belief, which prompted my writing this book, is that there is an immediate need for restoration of the constitutional principles that are debased by the current application of asset forfeiture laws. In my thinking, that requires passage by Congress of legislation commanding a complete overhaul of asset forfeiture law and the restoration of the right of private property.

1. The Crisis of Asset Forfeiture

The signers of the American Declaration of Independence, who staked their lives and fortunes on that courageous act, believed firmly that preeminent among our natural human rights is the right to own and enjoy private property.

Drawing upon the traditions of English common law and upon theories of political philosophers such as John Locke and Charles Louis de Montesquieu, the extraordinary men who later framed the U.S. Constitution regarded personal liberty as impossible to sustain without the enjoyment of this basic human right.[7] Typical American colonial beliefs were expressed in March of 1764 by Richard Henry Lee, who in the Virginia House of Burgesses spoke in opposition to the Crown, declaring that free possession of private property was one of the essential liberties of man.[8]

As a direct consequence of the practical American colonial experience with the despotism of the British Crown, the Fifth Amendment to the U.S. Constitution, part of our nation's Bill of Rights, declares:

> [No person shall] be deprived of life, liberty, or property, without due process of law; nor shall private property be taken for public use without just compensation.

Today, those historic words regarding the sanctity of property are mocked by daily events largely unknown to the general public, but starkly real to those who suffer in the insensitive grip of federal, state, and local law enforcement agencies engaged in the systematic degradation of the constitutional guarantee of property rights.

I refer to the horrendously unjust manner in which civil asset forfeiture laws are being applied by federal and state police and the courts. Those questionable official acts, which are literally robbing private citizens, depend for their dubious authority on musty legal doctrines dating from the dawn of the Republic and before. Arcane laws originally intended to protect customs revenues from the depredations of smugglers are now used by government to strip innocent Americans of their hard-earned property.

5

Those widespread injustices, and the misguided Gestapo-like zeal with which government agents are being allowed to perpetrate them, multiply daily all over America. Enlisted 25 years ago as a legitimate auxiliary tool in the so-called war on drugs, the legal doctrines of civil asset forfeiture have since been perverted to serve an entirely improper function in our democratic system of government—official confiscation from innocent citizens of their money and property with little or no due process of law or judicial protection.

Speaking both as a member of the bar since 1950 and as a public official sworn to uphold the Constitution, I share the concerns of Americans of all political persuasions, conservative to liberal, who believe this decidedly undemocratic trend is eroding civil rights and setting dangerous precedents for our nation's future.

Major Rights Endangered

Among my many apprehensions on this issue, here are concerns that stand out:

● **Civil rights are trampled.** Government abuse of asset forfeiture discriminates against minority Americans, especially African-Americans and Hispanics. Their often meager property and cash are seized at a far greater rate than that of whites because those minorities are said to fit stereotypical drug courier profiles prepared by insensitive police. In Memphis, 75 percent of the air travelers stopped by drug police were black, yet only 4 percent of the flying public is black.[9]

● **Billions are spent without controls.** Skirting safeguards provided by the normal governmental appropriations process, billions of dollars worth of property and hundreds of millions of dollars in cash fall into the hands of police and prosecutors, then are spent (and often misspent) with no control or oversight by elected legislative bodies—and little or no accounting to anyone, much less to the public.

● **Confiscation, but no crime.** In more than 80 percent of asset forfeiture cases the property owner is not even charged with a crime, yet the government officials can and usually do keep the seized property.[10]

● **A flimsy standard of proof.** To justify its seizure of property, whether it be your wallet or your house, government need only present evidence of what its agents see as "probable cause"[11]—the same minimal standard required to obtain a search warrant, which allows police only to seek evidence of a crime, not to permanently take property. Even worse, under asset forfeiture law the greater burden of proof is imposed on the property owner, who must establish by a "preponderance of the evidence" that his or her property has not been used in a criminal act.[12] Once a government agent shows "probable cause" to take your property, it is kept without further justification, whether or not a crime was committed. Often "probable cause" is mere rumor, gossip, a police hunch, or self-serving statements from anonymous paid police informants, from criminals cooperating in order to obtain a lighter sentence on pending charges, or from incarcerated convicts trying to shorten an existing jail term.

- **Punishment does not fit the crime.** There is little or no proportionality between the crimes alleged and the punishment imposed, raising a question, as the U.S. Supreme Court has now recognized, about what constitutes "excessive fines"—as prohibited by the Eighth Amendment.[13] Under asset forfeiture, hotels have been taken because gangs used them for drug transactions.[14] Apartment houses have been confiscated because drug deals allegedly took place in some apartments.[15] Three fraternity houses at the University of Virginia were seized by local police based on alleged sales of small quantities of drugs by student frat members.[16] At one point, under a federal drug enforcement policy known as "zero tolerance," the oceanographic research vessel *Atlantis* was seized off the coast of Massachusetts because of the discovery of a single marijuana cigarette in the ship's crew quarters.[17] Similarly, in California, a Scripps Oceanographic Institute research vessel was seized because a marijuana "roach" was found in the locker of a sailor who had long before been fired.[18]

Under such unreasonable applications of the law, nothing is safe from government seizure: not homes, boats, airplanes, gambling casinos, banks, dormitories at Harvard or Yale—not even the House of Representatives Post Office, the scene of cocaine dealing by clerks a few years ago.

- **Guilt by ownership.** The basic American presumption, innocent until proven guilty, has not only been reversed but property owners are now being forced to serve as police agents expected to incriminate others. Think what this could mean to you: your teenager is allowed to use the family car and a "roach" discarded in an ashtray by one of his passengers could cost you your car. Property owners who lease apartments, cars, or boats risk losing their valuable property because of

7

renters' conduct, over which the owner has no control—and sometimes, by law, can have no control.

- **Commercial chaos.** Under the theory of civil forfeiture, once an offending use is made of property, title to that property *immediately* passes to the government! Until the Supreme Court in 1993 approved some limitations on this theory,[19] subsequent innocent purchasers of the so-called tainted property could have it confiscated at any time, regardless of the buyer's lack of knowledge about the alleged illegal prior use. Similarly, unsecured creditors, lenders, mechanics, and suppliers can lose their valuable interests in such properties with little or no recourse. Exactly this scenario occurred in the case of a New York financier accused by the U.S. Department of Justice of business fraud; he agreed to government forfeiture of a corporate empire including a car dealership, real estate holdings, a gold mine, and many other legitimate enterprises—with no regard for the unsecured rights of numerous creditors who were owed millions of dollars for legitimate goods and services rendered to the accused's businesses prior to government seizure.[20] (This is the third largest federal civil forfeiture case, the only larger ones being "junk bond king" Michael Milken's forfeiture of $900 million to the Securities and Exchange Commission, and the Bank of Commerce and Credit International's forfeiture of $500 million to U.S. depositors.)[21]

- **Perverted procedures.** Procedural due process is almost totally lacking in asset forfeiture cases. Instead, the judicial system is stacked against innocent citizens and in favor of government. If property owners are unable to afford an attorney, as may be the case with inner-city homeowners, they are out of luck. Unlike indigent criminal defendants, they are not entitled to a government-appointed attorney. To contest the government's forfeiture, owners are allowed only 10 days in which to file a claim and post a 10 percent cash bond based on the value of the property. Even if the owner is successful in getting the property returned, the government is not liable for damage, storage, or other charges. As the *Chicago Tribune* editorialized on April 1, 1993, "A growing number of innocent parties . . . are being swept up in the net [of forfeiture]. And those who are unfairly trapped find that forfeiture laws turn due process on its head."

- **Questionable official conduct.** Perhaps worst of all, some police and prosecutorial authorities are engaging in questionable conduct themselves, guided by a profit motive because, under forfeiture, the property and cash expropriated from private citizens go directly to the government agents. The more they seize, the more they get for their own "official use." Former New York City police commissioner Patrick Murphy's 1992 testimony before Congress admitted that "[t]he large monetary value of forfeitures . . . has created a great temptation for state and local police departments to target assets rather than criminal activity."[22] How does this kind of activity differ from the despotic way in which the British Crown's hated admiralty courts operated in colonial America?

Lest you think the value of all this confiscated property is negligible, consider this: between 1985 and 1993 the U.S. Department of Justice took in over $3.2 billion from forfeitures.[23] In 1993 the total was $556 million.[24] The department had on hand an inventory of over 27,000 forfeited properties (real estate, businesses, vehicles, etc.) valued at $1.9 billion.[25] During 1993 the U.S. Customs Bureau seized property valued in excess of $611 million.[26] These figures do not include the billions of dollars of property taken by state and local government agencies.

As the authors of the *Pittsburgh Post-Gazette* series so aptly put it, "[t]he billions of dollars that forfeiture brings in to law enforcement agencies is so blinding that it obscures the devastation it causes the innocent."[27]

Expansion of Forfeiture Crimes

Not content with applying forfeiture law to drug offenses, legislators and prosecutors are rapidly expanding this principle to cover a host of alleged criminal acts in every area of activity. A growing number of states, including Texas and Florida, now apply civil forfeiture to *any* criminal activity (and in New Jersey any *alleged* criminal activity), which means owners must police their property against all possible criminal activity—or lose it.[28] In an attempt to curb savings and loan fraud, Congress in 1989 enacted a law making it a criminal offense to give false information on a loan application; as applied, the law is being used to confiscate property bought with the loan proceeds, even years later, and even if all payments are up to date.[29]

Under this provision of the law the U.S. Marshals Service seized $11 million of property, including five Choice Food convenience stores, a multiplex movie theater, and a consumer electronics store in Florida in 1991.[30] The same year, state authorities and agents of the U.S. Fish and Wildlife Service penetrated 15 miles onto a Texas ranch and seized a pickup truck belonging to the owner whom they wrongly accused of poisoning bald eagles. (It took him nine months to get the truck back although he was never charged with any crime).[31] Asset forfeiture is now being applied to the property of doctors and other health care professionals suspected of fraud related to Medicare and Medicaid programs, allowing even the seizure of patients' private medical records. Similar criminal provisions were included in President Clinton's ill-fated Health Security Act, allowing jail sentences, fines, and forfeiture of any property facilitating such health care "crimes."[32]

As you see, there are endless possibilities for any one of us to be caught in the snare of government forfeiture.

Destroying Liberty—And Life

To allow consideration of the human dimension in what is happening, one of my major aims in this book will be to convert abstract complaints about destruction of legal rights into the cruel reality of asset forfeiture. My purpose is to show you the way in which forfeiture law actually overwhelms the lives of average, innocent American citizens. I believe this factual demonstration is especially important because the common—and patently false—defense offered by federal and state officials supporting such laws is that the complaints of unjust treatment are only "aberrations," certainly not typical of the way in which the laws are generally administered.

This was the view of George Terwillinger III, associate attorney general in charge of the U.S. Department of Justice's asset forfeiture program during the administration of President George Bush. Mr. Terwillinger defended forfeiture by admitting only that in some few cases "dumb judgment" might have created problems for individual property owners. "That's why we have the courts," he said.[33] A similar defensive line was followed by Cary Copeland, director of the Justice Department's Executive Office of Asset Forfeiture under President Clinton, who blames forfeiture opposition on defense attorneys who "aren't interested in justice. They are interested in dismantling the program that takes money out of their pockets."[34]

Such cavalier official statements would have you believe that average Americans are not suffering because of asset forfeiture, that only "fat cat" drug "kingpins" are the victims of the law, as legislators intended. On June 22, 1993, Elvin Martinez, a member of the Florida House of Representatives and one of the drafters of that state's forfeiture law, testified before the U.S. House of Representatives

Subcommittee on Government Operations. Rep. Martinez contended the police administrators of the Florida law had corrupted its legislative purpose and were instead using it to harass "innocent owners" with little or no financial or other ability to defend themselves.[35] Statistics support this view, showing that the vast majority of forfeitures involve the property of average citizens caught in the clutches of this draconian law and its too-eager enforcers. For example, figures released by the U.S. Drug Enforcement Agency for the 18 months ending in December 1990 showed that only 17 percent of the 25,297 items (ranging from bank accounts to buildings) seized by DEA were valued in excess of $50,000.[36] Such figures speak volumes about the targets—and victims—of this law.

An American Police State?

In these pages I will discuss many specific examples of government forfeiture actions that have had terrible consequences, including death, for many innocent Americans. Here is just a representative sample of such stories:

• Willie Jones, the owner of a landscaping service, is an African-American. On February 27, 1991, he paid for an airplane ticket in cash at the Nashville, Tennessee, Metro Airport. This "suspicious" behavior—a black man paying cash—caused the ticket agent to alert Nashville police.[37] A police search of Jones and his luggage yielded no drugs. In his wallet, however, he did have $9,600 in cash on which a sniffing police dog detected traces of drugs (a chemical condition true of 97 percent of all U.S. currency now in circulation). The cash was promptly seized, despite protestations by Mr. Jones that he intended to use the money to purchase plants and shrubbery from growers in Houston, Texas, the destination for which he had purchased his round-trip plane ticket. No arrest was made. The seizure, however, nearly drove Mr. Jones out of business. He was unable to post the 10 percent bond money ($960) necessary to mount a legal challenge, so the DEA refused to return his cash. His only recourse was to sue the DEA for discrimination based on race. In April 1993, more than two years later, a federal judge ordered his $9,600 returned, noting that the presence of drug traces on currency is so prevalent as to be meaningless as a justification for forfeiting cash.[38]

• On April 9, 1989, Jacksonville, Florida, university professor Craig Klein's new $24,000 sailboat was "inspected" in what turned out to be a fruitless drug search by U.S. Customs Service agents. In the seven-hour rampage, the boat was damaged beyond repair. Using axes, power drills, and crowbars, agents dismantled the engine, ruptured the fuel tank, and drilled more than 30 holes in the hull, half of them below the waterline. Yet the Customs Service refused to compensate Klein, who was forced to sell the boat for scrap. Through the efforts of my colleague, former Rep. Charles Bennett of Florida, Congress passed a private claim bill granting Klein $8,900, small recompense for his economic loss and the efforts he was forced to make to preserve his liberty.[39]

• For years Billy Munnerlyn and his wife Karon owned and operated a successful air charter service out of Las Vegas, Nevada. In October 1989, Mr. Munnerlyn was hired for a routine job—flying Albert Wright, identified as a "businessman," from Little Rock, Arkansas, to Ontario, California. When the plane landed, DEA agents seized Mr. Wright's luggage and the $2.7 million inside. Both he and Mr. Munnerlyn were arrested. The DEA confiscated the airplane, the $8,500 charter fee for the flight, and all of Munnerlyn's business records. Although drug trafficking charges against Mr. Munnerlyn were quickly dropped for lack of evidence, the government refused to release his airplane. (Similar charges against Mr. Wright—who, unbeknownst to Munnerlyn, was a convicted cocaine dealer—were eventually dropped as well.) Mr. Munnerlyn spent over $85,000 in legal fees trying to get his plane back, money raised by selling his three other planes. A Los Angeles jury decided his airplane should be returned because they found Munnerlyn had no knowledge Wright was transporting drug money—only to have a U.S. district judge reverse the jury verdict. Munnerlyn eventually was forced to settle with the government, paying $7,000 for the return of his plane. He then discovered DEA agents had caused about $100,000 of damage to the aircraft. Under federal law the agency cannot be held liable for damage. Unable to raise enough money to restart his air charter business, Munnerlyn had to declare personal bankruptcy. He is now driving a truck for a living.[40]

• Police found 500 marijuana plants growing on a retiree's 37-acre farm in Kentucky. Delmar Puryear, who had retired with a disability and could not farm, insisted that he knew nothing about the plants. A jury apparently believed him, finding him innocent of state criminal charges. Despite this acquittal, the federal government refused to drop its efforts to seize the farm until Puryear agreed to pay $12,500.[41]

• Michael Sandsness and his wife, Christine, owned two gardening supply stores called "Rain & Shine" in Eugene and Portland, Oregon. Among the items sold were metal halide grow lights, used for growing many indoor plants. The grow lights also can be used to grow marijuana, but it is not illegal to sell them. Because some area marijuana gardens raided by DEA had the lights, the agency began building a case to seize the gardening supply business. In early 1991, the DEA sent undercover agents to the stores to try to get employees to give advice on growing marijuana. Unsuccessful in those efforts, the agents then engaged an employee in conversation, asking advice on the amount of heat or noise generated by the lights, making oblique comments suggesting that they wanted to avoid detection and commenting about *High Times* magazine. They never actually mentioned marijuana. The employee then sold the agents grow lights. DEA raided the two stores, seizing inventory and bank accounts. Agents told the landlord of one of the stores that if he did not evict Sandsness, the government would seize his building. The landlord reluctantly complied. While the forfeiture case was pending, the business was destroyed. Mr. Sandsness was forced to sell the remaining unseized inventory in order to pay off creditors.[42]

• Kathy Schrama, accused of stealing UPS packages worth at most $500 from her neighbors' doorsteps in New Jersey, saw local police take away her home, two cars, and all her furniture—even the Christmas presents she had purchased for her 10-year-old son. She later pleaded guilty to theft and paid a $5,000 fine. Although her property was finally returned, she is suing the state for $75 million in damages.[43]

• On March 12, 1993, 37 separate U.S. Food and Drug Administration commando-style raids were conducted in 23 cities. The targets: the professional offices of doctors who prescribe holistic, herbal, vitamin, and other "health supplements" deemed suspect by the FDA. Inventories and patient records were seized.[44]

• A collage created by artist Judy Enright of Ann Arbor, Michigan, was seized by agents of the U.S. Fish and Wildlife Service because it contained feathers from migratory birds. She had gathered the feathers, for which their former owners presumably had no further use, in her own backyard and nearby woods. The ever-vigilant federal agents informed her that possession of such feathers violates the 1918 Migratory Bird Treaty and its implementation law.[45]

Death by Bureaucrat

We will end this sample with the most shocking story of all. In Malibu, California, at a little before 9:00 a.m. on October 2, 1992, 61-year-old millionaire Donald Scott was shot dead in front of his wife when 30 local, state, and federal agents burst into his home and attempted to serve him with a search warrant enabling them to inspect his 200-acre Trail's End ranch for suspected cultivation of marijuana. Dressing upstairs, Scott was responding to his wife's screams for help, brandishing a handgun as he descended the stairs during the confusion of the raid.

After a five-month investigation, Ventura County district attorney Michael Bradbury concluded that the police, including the Los Angeles county sheriff's deputy who shot Scott to death, had slight evidence of drug cultivation, which proved ultimately to be false, and that the affidavits police gave the judge in support of the warrant request contained misstatements and omissions, which made the warrant invalid.[46]

Nicholas Gutue, the executor of Scott's estate, noted that Scott was known to be "fanatically antidrug." But he also noted that Scott had repeatedly refused to sell his $5 million scenic ranch to the U.S. National Park Service, which wanted to add the land to the adjacent Santa Monica Mountains National Recreation Area. U.S. Park Service officers took part in the combined county, state, and federal police raid, even though they had no legal jurisdiction to do so. Bradbury's investigation discovered that, at the final police briefing just before the raid, the possible government seizure of Scott's ranch was discussed; that documents reviewed at an earlier meeting included a property appraisal statement and a parcel map showing adjacent land sales in the area; and that two Los Angeles County sheriff's deputies from the forfeiture unit went along on the raid. This interest in confiscation of the Scott ranch was also borne out in documents uncovered by reporters for CBS television's *60 Minutes*, which aired a segment on the raid on April 5, 1993. The Ventura County district attorney concluded:

> We find no reason why law enforcement officers who were investigating suspected narcotics violation would have any interest in the value of the ... ranch or the value of property

sold in the same area other than if they had a motive to forfeit the property.

The report also stated that "[i]t is the District Attorney's opinion that the Los Angeles County Sheriff's Department was motivated, at least in part, by a desire to seize and forfeit the ranch for the government."

All this because forfeiture law admits of the possibility of the confiscation of a citizen's homestead. What greater evidence of the perversion of government power could there be?

* * *

These representative stories, chosen from among thousands, are the tip of the proverbial iceberg, but they clearly demonstrate the need for immediate reform of federal and state forfeiture laws.

2. How We Got into This Mess

To understand fully how the bizarre havoc currently caused by civil asset forfeiture laws can occur in a free country such as ours, one must search far back into the musty pages of Anglo-American history and law.

Civil asset forfeiture is premised on an archaic and curious legal fiction that personifies property. Bizarre as it may seem to the modern mind, this "personification theory" holds that an object can commit a wrong and be held guilty for its misdeeds. Therefore, it is argued, property may be subject to punishment. That punishment is forfeiture.

The Goring Ox Begets the Deodand

It is difficult today to comprehend how logical people (even long-dead English lawyers) could actually believe inanimate objects or animals could be capable of committing punishable acts. But this odd concept is more than a relic of our pagan, animist past. In the Old Testament, the Bible instructs us:

> When an ox gores a man or a woman to death, the ox must be stoned; the flesh may not be eaten. The owner of the ox, however, shall go unpunished.[47]

The implication is that an ox can be a moral agent, a being with the will and intent to do wrong, thus requiring retribution based on its evil acts.[48] According to the Talmudic interpretation of this passage, the command prohibits anyone receiving benefit from the offending animal ("flesh may not be eaten"). At the same time, that interpretation does not contemplate an exception that would allow a government agency to benefit.[49]

In both ancient Athens and the pre-Christian Roman Empire, the property of the ruler's political opposition was routinely confiscated.[50] There is historical evidence of an established pre-Judeo-Christian concept that held that an instrument of death itself must be accused and atonement exacted.[51]

17

However, leave it to our English forebears to go the Bible one better in their application of this peculiar notion. The English medieval law of "deodand" (from the Latin phrase *Deo Dandum*, meaning "to be given to God")[52] held that when an inanimate object or an animal caused the death of a person—say, a domestic animal killed a child—that object was automatically forfeited to the Crown as a deodand. In a sense this was a response to the superstition that a dead soul would not rest until its death was avenged.[53] The deodand was to be disposed of by the sovereign for the good of the deceased person's soul. It might be sold and the proceeds then used as Church offerings, to have a Mass said for the victim. One can safely assume that any profit from the sale went to the royal treasury. In fact, the deodand rapidly took on the double purpose of religious expiation and forfeiture, or "amercement," similar to other exactions of the Crown aimed at raising revenues rather than at saving souls.[54]

For the royal deodand collectors, the guilt or innocence of the object's owner in relation to the accident had little or no relevance to the forfeiture of the property. In effect, the English tradition viewed the property itself as "guilty" of the crime and the royal forfeiture was tantamount to an "arrest" of the object. In English common law, the procedure used by the Court of the Exchequer on behalf of the Crown against the object came to be known as an *in rem* proceeding (literally, in Latin, "against the thing").[55] The object was personified and declared "tainted" or evil, a continuing stigma the property could not evade, regardless of subsequent ownership.[56]

Outlawry and Corruption of Blood

There were also other deodand and property-related crimes under English common law. Any person found guilty of treason could suffer "attainder," that is, his civil rights were revoked and all his property forfeited to the Crown. Convicted felons forfeited only chattels to the Crown; real property escheated (reverted) to the local lord. A corollary legal consequence for the felon's heirs was loss of all right to their ancestor's property—a gory doctrine known as "corruption of blood."[57]

Allied with this quaint thinking was the brutal concept of "outlawry," which encouraged anyone to kill a fleeing felon—the reward being the right to take control of the dead man's property. Both the felon and the property were said to be "outside the law."[58]

During the Middle Ages, the concept of outlawry was broadened by the English Crown and used to crush political opponents, revoking a person's civil and property rights at the royal whim. After the Battle of Hastings in 1066, as the Norman Conquest engulfed England, the French learned from the vanquished; those who resisted were routinely declared "outlawed" and their property confiscated. In time, this ruthless process of outlawry became an instrument of native English political terror aimed at any suspected enemies—individuals were simply declared outlaws and put to death and their property taken without compensation.[59]

Like any government excess, this widespread abuse led to broad opposition, since peasants and nobility alike were threatened. When the barons at Runnymede forced King John to sign the Magna Carta in 1215, that historic document reflected the successful opposition to this specific abuse of power by the Crown, stating in part, "[n]o free man shall be . . . outlawed or exiled . . . except by the law of the land."[60]

For 400 years the Magna Carta put a stop to political outlawry, until 1610 during the reign of James I. King James seized private lands in Northern Ireland and turned them over to Scottish and English settlers. When the Irish rebelled in 1641, the British Parliament formally granted ownership of 75 percent of Ireland to English landlords. Dispossessed Scottish and Irish landowners were deported to the Caribbean and forced to work as slaves, the beginning of an English royal policy of banishment, exile, and property seizure lasting until 1715.

Long after the Crown ended political outlawry and its attendant property confiscation in England, criminal outlawry—revocation of all civil and property rights—remained as an auxiliary punishment after formal conviction of a crime against the sovereign, last occurring in this traditional use in 1859. Not until 1938 was the practice of criminal outlawry officially abolished in England, and in Scotland in 1949. It has never been repealed in Northern Ireland.[61]

It is not an overstatement to say that the pernicious and eccentric doctrines of deodand, outlawry, and *in rem* personification of property are the direct ancestors of modern American civil forfeiture. But like most Anglo-American legal traditions whose origins are obscured by the mists of time, those legal notions live on in formalized modern patterns because they still have some utility to those who control the government. Unfortunately, those same ancient concepts in modern dress are being used for new despotic ends, not only because the laws encoding them have never been repealed but because their expansion has been embraced with enthusiasm by too many contemporary American legislators and courts.

Admiralty: Wellspring of Modern Forfeiture

At this point we must consider English admiralty law, the immediate wellspring of American civil asset forfeiture law and procedure. Admiralty law, which governs all maritime matters relating to navigation and commercial sea traffic, is also firmly rooted in the English fiction that invests inanimate objects (in this case vessels) with both life and personal responsibility. In fact, modern American forfeiture statutes require the use of admiralty procedure in forfeiture cases.[62]

Throughout American history (at least until the inception of the current war on drugs) government forfeiture of property was a highly unpopular concept, principally because forfeiture was widely abused by the British Crown in its attempt to tax, control, and punish American colonists. "Writs of assistance" and "general warrants" were British legal devices allowing the Royal Navy to search colonial American ships and seize and forfeit them to the Crown.[63] The king's officers were particularly arrogant and arbitrary with American colonials when seizing property for forfeiture to the Crown. Americans accused of tax or customs duty evasion were remanded to special admiralty courts outside the regular judicial framework. The admiralty courts conducted trials by Crown officers whose pay and expenses came wholly from the fines and forfeitures they themselves adjudged. Jury trials were denied, and colonial protests against the basic conflict of interest in such a system were ignored.[64] One of the earliest cases of colonial rebellion came when the Crown seized John Hancock's schooner *Liberty* after he refused to pay the unpopular tax on its cargo of Madeira wine. Hancock, later president of the Continental Congress and first signer of the Declaration of Independence, was represented by Boston attorney John Adams, destined to be the second president of the United States, whose eloquent defense was used extensively by pamphleteers of the American Revolution. It was Adams who argued:

> Property is surely a right of mankind as real as liberty. The moment the idea is admitted into society that property is not sacred as the laws of God, and that there is not a force of law and public justice to protect it, anarchy and tyranny commence.[65]

This early American distrust of asset forfeiture is reflected not only in the property protection afforded by the Due Process Clause of the Fifth Amendment but in a specific limitation on forfeiture as a punishment for treason in Article III, which states:

> Congress shall have the power to declare the punishment for treason, but no attainder of treason shall work corruption of blood, or forfeiture except during the life of the person attainted.

British law provided for the seizure of felons' estates, a practice the first U.S. Congress forbade by the Act of April 30, 1790, which remains the law today.[66]

Nevertheless, forfeiture did find some use in the early United States as the first Congress adopted several maritime forfeiture laws, restricted to admiralty matters,[67] as civil sanctions against ships and cargo for failure to pay customs duties.[68] The U.S. Supreme Court generally upheld those early admiralty and customs forfeiture laws.[69]

Why did we Americans adopt English admiralty law, notwithstanding our rightful sensitivity to English barbarisms, especially property forfeiture? The reason for even a limited embrace was simple— government's eternal need for money. In the early years of our Republic, before federal income taxes were even a bad dream, import duties constituted over 80 percent of all federal revenues.[70]

In addition to the need for revenue, there were other practical reasons that explain why the young United States followed English admiralty law. A century later, Justice Oliver Wendell Holmes noted that "a ship is the most living of inanimate things. . . . Everyone gives a gender to vessels. . . . It is only by supposing the ship to have been treated as if endowed with personality, that the arbitrary seeming peculiarities of the maritime law can be made intelligible."[71]

Justice Holmes used this example:

> A collision takes place between two vessels, the Ticonderoga and the Melampus, through the fault of the Ticonderoga alone. That ship is under a lease at the time, the lessee has his own master in charge, and the owner of the vessel has no manner of control over it. The owner, therefore, is not to blame, and he cannot even be charged on the ground that the damage was done by his servants. He is free from personal liability on elementary principle. Yet it is perfectly settled that there is a lien on his vessel for the amount of the damage done, and this means that the vessel may be arrested and sold to pay the loss

in any admiralty court whose process will reach her. If a livery-stable keeper lets a horse and wagon to a customer, who runs a man down by careless driving, no one would think of claiming a right to seize the horse and the wagon.[72]

Holmes sees the rationale here:

> The ship is the only security available in dealing with foreigners, and rather than send one's own citizens to search for a remedy abroad in strange courts, it is easy to seize the vessel and satisfy the claim at home, leaving the foreign owners to get their indemnity as they may be able.[73]

Thus, one of the earliest influences on American civil forfeiture law is found in the maritime law of imperial Britain.

War and Prohibition

During the Civil War forfeiture was used by the U.S. government to confiscate the property of both Southern rebels and their sympathizers.[74] When Congress passed the Confiscation Act on July 17, 1862, authorizing *in rem* procedures against rebel property, the Supreme Court upheld it as part of broad military powers, stating:

> The power to declare war involves the power to prosecute it by all means and in any manner in which war may be legitimately prosecuted. It therefore includes the right to seize and confiscate all property of the enemy and dispose of it at the will of the captor.[75]

It is noteworthy that the Court upheld the law only because it was a war powers exercise aimed at enemies of the Union; the justices unanimously stated that if the purpose of the Confiscation Act were to punish an individual for treason or other criminal offenses, it would be unconstitutional because it substituted *in rem* civil procedures for a criminal trial, which would afford a defendant the protections of the Fifth and Sixth Amendments. Since the purpose was not to hold a person criminally liable but to speed the end of the war, "the provisions made to carry out the purpose, viz., confiscation, were legitimate, unless applied to others than enemies."[76] A few years later the Supreme Court restated this view, holding that if forfeiture of property, even though civil in nature, were actually based on offenses committed by the accused owner, the defendant would be entitled to protections against self-incrimination and illegally obtained evidence, which would apply in a criminal trial.[77]

22

During the Prohibition era in America, from 1919 to 1933, Congress extended civil asset forfeiture to include criminal violations of the Volstead Act and other laws governing the production, importation, and consumption of alcoholic beverages. Forfeiture was limited, however, to those portions of real property actually used for the illegal production of alcoholic beverages.[78] As for chattels, in 1921 the Supreme Court upheld the forfeiture of an auto dealer's secured interest in a vehicle used to transport illegal alcohol, even though the car had been sold to a bona fide purchaser and the dealer had no involvement in the crime.[79]

From this brief historical review one can reasonably conclude that American forfeiture law, however limited its application until recent years, had a life of its own, distinct from the original English idea of the Crown's deodand. If there is a consistent theme in the American experience with this concept, it is that our leaders periodically sought to employ forfeiture to achieve certain defined contemporary political and social goals, either good or ill: financing the operations of the early federal government; preserving the Union of States from rebellion; trying to remove from the American people the right to have a shot of bourbon or a bottle of cold beer.

The War on Drugs

Against this background, we turn now to the full flowering of civil asset forfeiture in America—as a tool in the war to banish what lawmakers have chosen to call "controlled dangerous substances," that is, drugs or other substances the manufacture, distribution, or possession of which has been made illegal by acts of Congress or state legislatures.

As we have seen, forfeiture was rarely used in America until the 1980s, but since then it has flourished, first as a weapon in the arsenal of the drug war,[80] more recently in combatting a host of other criminal acts. In fact, during the first 10 years that federal drug forfeiture powers were available, they were rarely used by law enforcement officials. This lack of use prompted the General Accounting Office to issue a 1981 report entitled "Asset Forfeiture—A Seldom Used Tool in Combatting Drug Trafficking," which was instrumental in increasing the volume and scope of property confiscation.[81]

Today, there are over 100 different federal forfeiture statutes, addressing a wide range of matters both criminal and civil. Those statutes extend from the forfeiture of animals seized from animal-fighting impresarios (cockfighting)[82] and contraband cigarettes seized from interstate smugglers[83] to firearms violations[84] and property ill-gotten from violations of RICO (the Racketeer Influenced and Corrupt Organizations Act).[85]

Federal government agencies with statutory forfeiture power include not only the Drug Enforcement Administration and the U.S. Customs Bureau of the Treasury Department, but also the FBI; the U.S. Coast Guard; the U.S. Postal Service; the Bureau of Land Management and the Fish and Wildlife Bureau of the Interior Department (as the feather-collecting Ms. Enright knows only too well); the Securities and Exchange Commission; the Department of Health and Human Services; the Food and Drug Administration; the Justice Department, including the Immigration and Naturalization Service; the Department of Housing and Urban Development; and, of course, the Internal Revenue Service. In addition, more than 3,000 state and local police departments exercise forfeiture powers. In New Jersey—a state that has adopted one of the country's most severe forfeiture laws, triggered by *any* alleged criminal conduct—forfeiture is used even against shoplifters.[86]

Basic Federal Forfeiture Law

The Comprehensive Drug Abuse Prevention and Control Act of 1970 contains the basic federal anti-drug civil asset forfeiture provisions. It provides for the forfeiture of

> [a]ll controlled substances which have been manufactured, distributed, dispensed, or acquired ... [a]ll raw materials, products, and equipment ... which are used, or intended for use, in manufacturing ... delivering, importing, or exporting any controlled substance[s] ... property which is used, or intended for use, as a container for [forfeitable controlled substances] ... [a]ll conveyances, including aircraft, vehicles, or vessels, which are used, or intended for use, to transport, or in any manner to facilitate the transportation, sale, receipt, possession or concealment [of such controlled substances].[87]

In 1978, the act was amended to provide for forfeiture of

> [a]ll moneys ... or other things of value furnished or intended to be furnished by any person in exchange for a controlled substance ... all proceeds traceable to such an exchange. ...[88]

In 1984, the act was amended to provide for forfeiture of

> [a]ll real property . . . which is used, or intended to be used, in any
> manner or part, to commit, or to facilitate the commission of . . .
> a violation.[89]

There is an important progression of events here that must be recognized. The 1970 Comprehensive Drug Abuse Prevention and Control Act provided for the forfeiture of property used in connection with controlled substances. The 1978 Psychotropic Substances Act added forfeiture of money and other things of value furnished or intended to be furnished in exchange for a controlled substance and all proceeds traceable to such an exchange. The 1984 Comprehensive Crime Control Act added all real property used or intended to be used to commit or to facilitate the commission of a drug crime.

But the progression did not end in 1984. The 1986 Anti-Drug Abuse Act expanded civil forfeiture to include the proceeds of money-laundering activity.[90] Certain 1990 amendments to that act included proceeds traceable to counterfeiting and other offenses affecting financial institutions—a bow to the savings and loan scandals.[91] Then in 1992 Congress added more categories of offenses[92] and also covered proceeds traceable to motor vehicle theft.[93]

Perhaps the most dramatic expansion of basic forfeiture law came in 1992 with the adoption of a statute that applies

> in any forfeiture *in rem* in which the subject property is cash,
> monetary instruments in bearer form, funds deposited in an
> account in a financial institution . . . or other fungible
> property.[94]

Under this provision the government is not required to identify the specific property in the offense that is the basis for forfeiture but may seize "any identical property found in the same place or the same account as the property involved in the offense," which might have been forfeitable had it remained in the same place or account.[95]

All this recent statutory expansion means not only a dramatic increase in the number of crimes covered by civil asset forfeiture but also a significant lessening of any relationship between an owner's guilty act or offense, if any, and the property that is subjected to forfeiture.

Prompted largely by the war on drugs, this distinctly American forfeiture policy, wisely or unwisely, is now far removed from the ancient notion of "arresting" "guilty" or "tainted" property "accused" of causing a wrong. And yet for the most part, the original ancient judicial procedures used for forfeitures govern this whole new federal apparatus, often much to the detriment of individual constitutional rights, and the delight of those in and out of government who benefit from wholesale confiscation of billions of dollars worth of private property.

About Criminal Forfeiture

Before going further, it is appropriate to note the important distinctions between civil asset forfeiture, the topic of my greatest concern, and criminal forfeiture.

The term "forfeiture" has been defined legally as the "loss of some right or property as a penalty for some illegal act."[96] As I have described, the current administration of *civil* forfeiture law allows government confiscation of property with no need to prove personal guilt, or even charge the owner with any wrongdoing.

Criminal forfeiture, on the other hand, arises under criminal statutes that allow *in personam* actions against a named criminal defendant. In such cases, forfeiture comes about subsequent to and as a punitive consequence of the defendant's conviction for specific criminal acts, usually as a supplement to other statutory punishment including possible incarceration or fines.[97] I think most fair-minded observers believe criminal forfeiture is justifiable as a criminal punishment.[98] The important difference in this procedure, compared to civil forfeiture, is that criminal forfeiture occurs, at least in theory, only after a trial of the defendant at which full constitutional and procedural safeguards of due process apply.[99] No conviction; no forfeiture. No wrongdoing; no property confiscation. The issue at trial is the individual's misconduct, not the fictional guilt of an inanimate object, as in civil forfeiture cases.

For a criminal forfeiture to take place, there first must be a criminal conviction, where the burden is placed upon the government (as every Perry Mason fan knows well) to adduce proof "beyond a reasonable doubt." In a civil forfeiture action, as I have mentioned previously and will more fully explore, the government has the burden merely of showing probable cause, the easiest of all evidentiary standards to meet. The burden of proof then shifts to the property owner to show why his property should be returned.

It is not too much to say that if federal and state forfeiture authority were limited to criminal cases—in other words, if civil asset forfeiture were abolished—many of the worst excesses visited upon innocent property owners would be at an end. For property owners there would be the added constitutional protection of procedural due process in all its aspects. Most importantly, the burden of proof would rest with government prosecutors.[100]

Typical of this type of appropriately punitive criminal forfeiture statute is the RICO law to which I have already referred. The courts have had no hesitation in applying RICO's broad criminal forfeiture language as intended by Congress in order to end the power of criminals over American business and this has allowed the seizure of both illegally and legally acquired assets as punishment.[101] In that noncriminally acquired assets can be forfeited as punishment under RICO, this use of criminal forfeiture is in some respects potentially even broader in scope than civil forfeiture.

Although I support the proper use of criminal forfeiture laws, I am troubled by the breadth of application allowed by some courts. Under RICO, for example, a convicted defendant must forfeit any property interest, however legitimately it may have been acquired or employed, if that interest allows him to exercise influence over an alleged RICO "enterprise," which now has become a very broadly interpreted term—so much so that it has been held to encompass what I believe to be the legitimate conduct of those active in the national right-to-life movement, right down to peaceful picketing by anti-abortion protest-ers at abortion clinics.[102] This liberal view has the potential for far-reaching and dangerous consequences. Such forfeiture decisions can cause serious disruption to commercial life. A RICO defendant convicted of failure to pay a state sales tax due from his gas station franchise, for example, was ordered to forfeit not only an amount equal to what he owed in delinquent taxes and penalties but also 34 separate corporations.[103]

3. The Problem with the Police

Daniel Webster, one of the great congressional leaders in the decades prior to the Civil War, offered some sage advice for Americans that is still timely:

> Good intention will always be pleaded for every assumption of power. . . . [T]he Constitution was made to guard the people against the dangers of good intentions. There are men in all ages who mean to govern well, but they mean to govern. They promise to be good masters, but they mean to be masters.[104]

Webster's wise admonition should be kept in mind as we examine the disturbing role law enforcement agencies at all levels of government have come to play in asset forfeiture. There can be no doubt about it, civil forfeiture as practiced today is "big business" by any measure. While federal and state governments snatch billions of dollars in cash, personal property, and real estate under the guise of law enforcement, too often innocent property owners are the ones who "get the business," as the old saying goes.

In their unguarded moments, even the federal officials responsible for administering the forfeiture laws admit what is really going on. Michael F. Zeldin, director of the Justice Department's Asset Forfeiture Office under the Bush administration, told a 1993 conference on white-collar crime:

> We had a situation in which the desire to deposit money into the asset forfeiture fund became the reason for being of forfeiture, eclipsing in certain measure the desire to effect fair enforcement of the laws. . . .[105]

Federal and State Big Bucks

Prior to the adoption of the Comprehensive Crime Control Act of 1984, the money realized from federal civil forfeitures was deposited in the general fund of the U.S. Treasury. Now it goes primarily to the

29

Justice Department's Asset Forfeiture Fund and to the Treasury Department's Forfeiture Fund.[106] The money is then supposed to be used for forfeiture-related expenses and general law enforcement purposes, with no further necessity for congressional appropriations or authorization. This is where a grievous problem has arisen—law enforcement officials are allowed to keep all the proceeds from the property they confiscate, an invitation to uncontrollable abuse. Today, most of those billions are spent by the same authorities who confiscate the property, with little or no outside supervision or control—but with plenty of incentive to push more and more profitable forfeitures to the maximum.

The problem is worse on the state and local level, where the same officer who seizes a car can then use it on patrol. It goes without saying that allowing law enforcement agencies to keep any cash or property they confiscate creates a built-in conflict of interest of the first magnitude. In the opinion of Brenda Grantland, a defense attorney specializing in this area of law:

> This began the war on the private property of innocent Americans—not just the "proceeds of crime" or the assets of convicted criminals. Armed with statutory authorization ... and with no legislative oversight over how they spent it, the popularity of asset forfeiture immediately skyrocketed. This provision not only gave the police the power to terrorize innocent citizens—it also allowed the police to finance their own new police state out of the property they seized.[107]

The amount deposited in the U.S. Department of Justice Assets Forfeiture Fund increased from $27 million in fiscal year 1985, to $556 million in 1993.[108] Of the amount taken in 1993, $358 million was in cash and $156 million were proceeds from the disposal of forfeited property; $215 million of the total was returned to state and local law enforcement agencies that assisted in investigations leading to forfeitures.[109] And $25 million in forfeited property (planes, boats, cars, etc.) was pressed into official use by federal law enforcement agencies or transferred to state and local police for their use.[110] In 1993 the Justice Department had on hand an inventory in excess of 27,000 separate properties, ranging from luxury waterfront homes in Florida to crack houses in Philadelphia, with a combined value of more than $1.9 billion.[111] The U.S. Customs Service seized property with a value of over $726 million in fiscal year 1992,[112] including the entire Indian Wells Country Club, Resort Hotel, and 27-hole golf course in the southern California desert, and the 18-hole Royal Kenfield Golf Course in Las Vegas.[113]

Land of the Much Too Free

So attractive has the forfeiture of valuable real estate become to police that most departments have quietly adopted a policy of "structured arrests," making certain that undercover agents purchase drugs or make deals when they are physically located in a valuable building or on a high-priced tract of land—which then can be confiscated immediately by the police. The use of even a small part of a larger parcel of land as the locus of an alleged drug crime can render the entire tract subject to forfeiture, under the theory that the use of the land "facilitates" the commission of the crime.[114] Thus, the use of a car parked in a driveway in which the purchase of cocaine occurred rendered the entire house and land subject to forfeiture.[115] And when a drug transaction took place in an area including a driveway, house, and swimming pool, the government could seize all that area and 30 acres of adjoining land as well.[116]

Not even the dead can escape possible real estate forfeiture. Three months before he died of cancer at the age of 49, wealthy George Gerhardt, who had no criminal record, was the subject of a secret police informant's tip. The tipster claimed Gerhardt was paid $10,000 for the use of the boat dock at his $250,000 Fort Lauderdale, Florida, waterfront home where cocaine shipments were unloaded. The informant could not recall, however, the name of the boat, the date it happened, or even the dealers' names; thus, the government's legal brief stated that it "does not possess the facts necessary to be any more specific." Three months after he died, Gerhardt's heirs, who had inherited the family home, were ousted from the premises. The locks were changed and the government rented the house out for $2,200 a month. No warrant was ever issued for anyone's arrest; no charges were filed against any living person; yet on the basis of a secret informer, the house was taken.

Robyn Hermann, assistant U.S. attorney for the southern district of Florida, admitted the obvious—the purpose is "not so much to punish at this stage. The motivation really is to use the proceeds from the sale of the property to prevent other drug offenses."[117] As with Ms. Hermann's simplistic rationale, it is easy for police officials to offer superficial justifications for such massive seizures, usually accompanied by stern appeals for public support in the fight against drug lords and felons. But as I have pointed out, more than 80 percent of the 25,297 items of cash and property seized by the U.S. Drug Enforcement Agency from June 1989 to December 1990 were valued at less (usually much less) than $50,000.[118]

The Little Guy Pays

If any proof were needed that the majority of the people who suffer from civil asset forfeiture are average Americans, not rich criminals or even drug lords, it came in documents obtained under the state Freedom of Information Act by officials of the Michigan Association for the Preservation of Property (MAPP). In 1992, Michigan law enforcement agencies used civil forfeiture in 9,770 instances and confiscated an average of only $1,434 per seizure. A total of $14,007,227 in cash and property was seized, up from the 1991 total of $11,848,547. Property taken included 54 private homes (up from 29 homes in 1991) with an average value of $15,881 (this in a nation in which the average price of a home is now over $100,000). Autos seized totaled 807, with an average value of $1,412, not exactly luxury models. A total of 8,909 seizures produced $9,225,515 in cash and other negotiable instruments and only $2,754,818 in personal property. An examination of records showed seizures were often uncontested because the value of the cash or property confiscated in most cases was too low to justify the $5,000 to $10,000 in attorney fees and court costs such a challenge would require. Police argue there are so few contests because the owners are guilty of some crime and do not want to force the issue by challenging the forfeiture in court. Of the 123 separate police agencies reporting, however, only one, the Muskegon Police Narcotics Department, gave any detailed accounting of the number of arrests made. No police department gave any evidence of convictions associated with the forfeitures. The Muskegon police seized cash 72 times, totaling $31,199, with an average for each seizure of $433. Tom Flook, an official of MAPP, went to the heart of the matter: "[O]bviously, most civil forfeitures in Michigan are not much more than curbside shake-downs."[119]

In 1992, the Committee on Public Safety of the California State Assembly, a body firmly in control of the Democratic Party for many years, made this statement in a majority report on legislation aimed at curbing that state's asset forfeiture program:

> Asset forfeiture is a multi-million dollar source of revenue for [California] law enforcement. Thus, there is an incentive to seize property as a revenue source. . . . [P]ersons suspected of participation in or having knowledge of drug crimes rarely will be given the benefit of the doubt by those who will gain financially by the seizure. This is viewed as a particular problem in times of tight budgets.[120]

From the other end of the California political spectrum, Republican Assemblyman Charles Quackenbush said, "[t]o take property from people who haven't been convicted of anything is an outrageous abuse of police power." His colleague, Assemblyman David Knowles, one of the most conservative Republicans in the legislature, agreed:

> This isn't about law and order. This is an issue of property rights. This is about police kicking down people's doors and taking their money. It's tyrannical government run amok.[121]

One federal judge recently noted that the vast quantity and value of the assets seized by police under forfeiture laws rightly "leads some observers to question whether we are seeing fair and effective law enforcement or an insatiable appetite for a source of increased revenue."[122]

I believe that one of the main objectives of forfeiture reform must be to put an end to the "pillage and plunder" mentality of greed that dominates some law enforcement thinking, a direct product of the easy money temptation offered by the current civil asset forfeiture laws.

Not So Random Violence

Official conduct such as I have described might be easier to understand were it isolated and unrepresentative. But it is not. Events like those are widespread in every part of the United States. Nor are those subjected to such police activities usually wealthy people such as the late Donald Scott. The sad truth is that the vast majority of citizens affected by such police conduct are average people who happen to be in the wrong place at the wrong time—ironically, not unlike the victims of crime generally in this unfortunate day and age.

On the night of August 25, 1992, for example, in Poway, California, a U.S. Customs Service drug raid included numerous heavily armed DEA agents who broke down the door of Donald L. Carlson's suburban San Diego County home. Aroused from sleep and thinking a robbery was under way, he grabbed a gun as the agents smashed the door and lobbed a percussion grenade into his home. In an exchange of gunfire, Carlson was hit three times, in the arm, lung, and femoral vein. After six weeks on a ventilator in intensive care he was lucky to be alive. He will suffer lifelong diaphragm paralysis, chronic pain, and circulatory problems.

There were no drugs in Carlson's house, and for good reason. He has no criminal record, has never used illegal drugs, is a vice president of a Fortune 500 company, and is a family man respected by friends and associates. But Carlson was falsely fingered by a paid informer who had already been kicked out of one federal anti-drug program because he filed other false reports, one fingering a vacant house! After the shooting, Carlson's neighbors heard one agent tell another, "[n]ow get the story straight. He shot first." Mr. Carlson has filed suit for damages and alleges a government conspiracy to cover up the Customs Service blunder. No one has been charged with any wrong-doing as a result of this tragic event.[123]

Trouble in Paradise

Sympathetic people of limited means often lose everything in forfeiture cases. In 1991, for example, four years after a mentally unstable 28-year-old man was placed on probation after pleading guilty to growing marijuana in the backyard of his parents' home in Hawaii, where he lived, a Maui police detective was combing through old police records looking for possible forfeiture cases. For the Maui police, like other law enforcement agencies, forfeiture means immediate control of assets and money for the department to spend pretty much as it pleases. Because the parents admitted they knew their son was growing pot, even though they tried to get him to stop, the Maui police saw legal grounds on which to take their home. In February 1991, just under the five-year statute of limitations, the police began a civil forfeiture claim.

The father, Joseph Lopes, a 65-year-old retired sugar plantation worker, had worked for 30 years, living in rented company housing while saving to buy his own home. In 1987, when the son was arrested and placed on probation for the pot offense, forfeiture was rarely used by police. Honolulu Assistant U.S. Attorney Marshall Silverberg readily admitted that the government now sees an attractive financial payoff in forfeiture, and they use it. Police and prosecutors regularly comb through old case records looking for forfeiture possibilities. With a

34

remarkable touch of official arrogance, Silverberg told a reporter, "I concede the time lapse on this case is longer than most, but there was a violation of the law, and that makes this appropriate, not money-grubbing." Then with a supreme touch of charity (if not chutzpah), the government lawyer added, "[t]he other way to look at this, you know, is that the Lopeses could be happy we let them live there as long as we did."

The couple's attorney, Matthew Menzer, says he has eight other cases in which the police have gone back years, all cases involving small-time crimes that were resurrected for forfeiture actions. "Digging these cases out now is a business proposition, not law enforcement," says Menzer.[124]

Addicted to Forfeiture

As if on the narcotics they are supposed to control and suppress, law enforcement agencies at all levels have become addicted to forfeiture as a source of ready cash to supplement their budgets. A July 1990 U.S. Department of Justice bulletin sent to all U.S. attorneys warned about falling behind Justice budget goals:

> We must significantly increase forfeiture production to reach our budget target. Failure to achieve the $470 million projection would expose the Department's forfeiture program to criticism and undermine confidence in our budget predictions. Every effort must be made to increase forfeiture income in the three remaining months of fiscal year 1990.[125]

It also tells us something about Justice Department priorities when we see that in a previous bulletin, Acting Assistant Attorney General Edward Dennis, Jr., advised all U.S. attorneys that they were "expected to divert personnel from other activities," including criminal cases, in order to prepare all forfeiture cases for judicial action.[126]

Is it really more important to our national government to pursue money for its budget than to protect citizens against crime? Apparently so. Yet in March 1993, the *Las Vegas Review-Journal* reported that Cary Copeland, then the chief Justice Department forfeiture official, told an audience at the University of Nevada in Las Vegas, "[i]t is 'outrageous' to suggest the federal government would 'run amok' in search of only a few billion dollars, a fraction of 1 percent of its annual budget."[127]

Law Enforcement Purposes

The forfeiture provisions of the 1984 Comprehensive Crime Control Act require that money from property seizures be used only for law enforcement purposes.[128] Because federal forfeiture funds are shared with more than 3,000 state and local police agencies involved in forfeitures, it is impossible to oversee whether these funds are indeed used for "law enforcement purposes." Since 1985 there have been over 200,000 federal seizures of cash and property, and state and local police have reaped a windfall of over $1 billion as a result.

Where is all that money going?

New York: In Suffolk County, Long Island, District Attorney James M. Catterson controls all the property and cash resulting from forfeitures, a fact of which the county supervisors were unaware until revealed by the local daily, *Newsday.* Catterson drives a BMW 735i seized from a drug dealer, and used $3,412 from the forfeiture fund for mechanical and body work on "his" car, including $75 for pinstriping. Among other things, Catterson has authorized expenditures from the fund of $300 for a retirement gift watch for his secretary, and $3,999 for chairs. Catterson, whose office has not been audited by the county since 1981, told a reporter, "By my view, I really don't have to ask anyone else's permission to spend monies that come to me."[129]

New Jersey: Somerset County (southwest of Newark and north of Trenton) is 13th in population in the state, but number 1 in assets seized by forfeiture: in 1991, in cash alone, the police took in $1,029,341. The man who controls the money is County Prosecutor Nicholas Bissell, Jr. Among other unusual official activities, an arrested suspect, James Guiffre, was allegedly threatened with felony drug charges carrying 10 years in prison and forfeiture of his residence unless he signed over deeds to two parcels of land he had bought in 1988 for $174,000. Legal consultation for Guiffre was not part of the deal, and he did as he was told within 26 hours of his arrest. Several months later, the county sold the two lots for $20,000 to two friends of Bissell's chief of detectives, Richard Thornburg, who personally had forced the deal on Guiffre at the time of his arrest. Bissell also placed $300,000 from the forfeiture fund in a small bank (with deposits of $1.8 million) owned by Bissell's longtime business associate. In addition, he spent $6,000 from the fund to buy private tennis club memberships for his assistant prosecutors and police detectives.[130]

Rhode Island: In the quaint town of Little Compton (population 3,339), there are 7 police officers and there hasn't been a murder since 1965. But the police got $3 million from the federal forfeiture program and quickly ran out of "law enforcement purposes" for which to spend the loot. Soon there were more police cars than police officers, including new Pontiac Firebirds for the chief and his lieutenant, two high-tech cruisers equipped with video cameras, an animal control van, a four-wheel-drive Jeep, and a new 23-foot boat with pickup truck and trailer. They also built an indoor-outdoor firing range, a radio system tower with all new radio equipment, and a new police station costing $725,000, which they didn't need because they had just renovated their old one. They bought 14 guns ($400 each) and 9 bulletproof vests ($500 each), bought police radios for school buses, added overtime shifts so they could up the annual pay of each of the 7 officers by $7,000 in overtime, sent 3 officers to college, and set aside $500,000 for salary and benefits for the lieutenant.

Unfortunately, federal auditors who finally reviewed the spending spree determined that 73 percent of the expenditures were questionable, including $16,000 for a computer for the town treasurer, $15,000 for a truck for the maintenance department, and $17,000 for a wood chopper.[131]

Rip-Offs Coast to Coast

The *Los Angeles Times* reported in January 1992 that six Los Angeles County sheriff's narcotics officers went to trial on charges of "stealing hundreds of thousands of dollars in cash and property during drug raids, beating suspects, planting narcotics, and falsifying police reports."[132] In another trial in March 1992, two other of the same department's narcotics officers were charged with drug-money skimming, and the *Times* reported that Deputy Sheriff Eufasio G. Cortez testified that the money-skimming scandal began

> with narcotics officers taking "a few dollars off the top" to buy law enforcement equipment or dinner after a successful drug raid but quickly spread out of control.
>
> Narcotics officers . . . began stealing seized property including television sets, stereos and jewelry that had been confiscated during raids. . . . Before long officers were skimming hundreds of dollars, then thousands, in cash.[133]

In these and other trials, 12 L.A. County officers were convicted of various charges. A former L.A. sheriff's deputy, Robert Sobel, who was indicted and turned state's evidence, testified his narcotics unit stole $60 million in cash and property during 1988 and 1989 alone.[134]

In 1992, there were numerous reports of police stopping suspects on the street, confiscating any cash found on them, and then not reporting the forfeiture.[135] It has also been a Washington, D.C., police practice to seize autos of men accused of soliciting prostitutes; the cars are forfeited, even if the "johns" are acquitted. Arrests are usually made by undercover policewomen serving as "decoys."[136]

The Sheriff of Volusia County

One of the classic cases of police abuse of forfeiture powers occurred on a continuing basis in Volusia County (the Daytona Beach area) in northeastern Florida, which sits astride Interstate 95, the major East Coast north-south auto and truck route to Miami and southern Florida.

This scandal was first exposed in an investigative special report in the *Orlando Sentinel* in June 1992.[137] Reporters Jeff Brazil and Steve Berry discovered that Volusia County sheriff Bob Vogel had created a special police "drug squad" that literally preyed upon thousands of innocent motorists driving on I-95. Operating under the broadly written 1980 Florida Contraband Forfeiture Act—which allowed police seizure of cash and property based on "probable cause," without arrest, in suspected felony cases—the police were engaging in what can charitably be called highway robbery. Police conduct was guided by no written rules and reviewed by no one but Sheriff Vogel, who controlled all the funds confiscated. Any person stopped who possessed $100 or more in cash was to be assumed a drug trafficker under the sheriff's rules.

Here are a few of the facts uncovered by the *Sentinel:*

• In an analysis of more than a 1,000 traffic stops, more than 70 percent of the cars were driven by blacks or Hispanics.

• Of more than 500 auto searches, 80 percent had racial-minority drivers.

• Less than 1 percent of the drivers were given traffic tickets and only one in four was arrested, usually involving drug offenses. Ninety percent of the drivers from whom cash was confiscated without arrest were black or Hispanic.

• From 1989 until the adverse publicity in 1992, the squad seized almost $8 million in cash from motorists—and in only four cases did the innocent owners get all their money back! In any cases where money was returned to motorists, the sheriff always kept a substantial amount (10 to 50 percent) for "expenses."

It was a regular police practice to bargain with motorists on the spot—stopped on the side of I-95, taking part of their cash in exchange for agreement not to file claims for the cash or to take legal action against the sheriff's department or the police. Some drivers were stripped of their cash because they "looked like" drug suspects, one because he had no luggage, another because he had "too much" luggage. Carrying U.S. currency in denominations that the sheriff's deputies felt typical of drug dealers also caused confiscation—including $1, $10, $20, $50, and $100 bills! And the police repeatedly used the scientifically discredited excuse that illegal drug residue was found on the currency confiscated.[138]

Interestingly, the sheriff's "Selective Enforcement Team" rarely stopped vehicles traveling in the northbound lanes of I-95, those most likely to be carrying quantities of drugs to northern cities from southern Florida smuggling points. Instead, they concentrated on the southbound lanes, assuming this was where they would find people headed to southern Florida to buy drugs and their easily forfeitable cash—which the police confiscated. So much for sincere concern about "interdiction" and winning the "war on drugs."

Often when car occupants were considered "suspicious" by deputies, they were told to wait in a police patrol car where their conversation was secretly recorded by a hidden microphone. No warnings of suspects' legal rights were given because they were not under arrest, but the slightest remark that could be interpreted as supporting forfeiture for possible drug trafficking was used to justify confiscation of their money.

The tape of a suspect's patrol-car conversation on April 24, 1990, is particularly poignant. The suspects were Selena Washington, a 43-year-old Charleston, S.C., black woman and her 41-year-old cousin, John Washington. They had been stopped for speeding and a search of the car turned up $19,000 in cash, which Ms. Washington insisted was meant for the purchase of materials in Miami to repair her home and real estate properties damaged by the recent Hurricane Hugo. Such supplies were scarce and high priced in the Charleston area in the wake of the destructive storm, as she explained to the policeman. The police refused to make calls to verify her story and accused her of

39

being involved with drugs. They told her she would have to retain an attorney and have him seek return of the money. At one point on the tape, as the police searched her car, the obviously terrified Ms. Washington can be heard repeating over and over again the 23d Psalm: "The Lord is my shepherd. I shall not want. . . ."

Eight months later, in an out-of-court settlement, Ms. Washington's attorney succeeded in getting the sheriff's office to return $15,000, the police keeping $4,000. He advised her that challenging the forfeiture in court would cost more than the amount she sought to recover. His legal fee was $1,000. There was no evidence of any drug involvement and all aspects of her story checked out.

But Ms. Washington did not rest there. With the assistance of the National Association for the Advancement of Colored People in Washington, D.C., a class-action suit was filed on her behalf and that of other citizens whose cash had been confiscated by the Volusia County police. In the course of the pretrial proceedings in this suit, Volusia County deputy sheriff Richard Forrest said that a caricature of a black man and a directive listing ethnic characteristics of "drug couriers" had been distributed to deputies by the sheriff. Other police concurred that such ethnic descriptions had been used to train police.[139]

In August 1994, it was revealed that Sheriff Vogel had spent at least $205,826 of county funds paying an Orlando law firm, largely to defend him and his department against two lawsuits, one by Ms. Washington. In August, he also made a $7,500 down payment to former U.S. assistant attorney general and Watergate prosecutor Jon Sale, now in Miami, to defend him in a U.S. Department of Justice investigation of the I-95 cash seizures. The department wants to know whether the civil rights of those involved were violated.[140]

Elsewhere in America

Lest you think the Volusia County experience was a one-time aberration among law enforcement agencies, consider the case of Eagle County in the northwest corner of Colorado. There, in the beautiful Rocky Mountains, on a 60-mile stretch of Interstate 70 during 1989 and 1990, more than 500 drivers were stopped. The reason, as two deputies testified in a federal class-action suit, was because the drivers were black or Hispanic. The sheriff's office there also created a profile of "drug couriers" based on race, ethnicity, and out-of-state auto license plates. In ruling that this tactic was unconstitutional, U.S. district court judge Jim Carrigan said:

> If this nation were to win its war on drugs at the cost of sacrificing its citizens' constitutional rights, it would be a Pyrrhic victory indeed. If the rule of law rather than the rule of man is to prevail, there cannot be one set of search and seizure rules applicable to some and a different set applicable to others.[141]

It might even be of some comfort to learn that the Volusia County experience I have described was unique in the state of Florida, but sadly it is not. Even before Sheriff Vogel perfected his I-95 shakedown operation, other Florida police authorities were hard at work using the 1980 state forfeiture law to strip innocent citizens of cars, planes, boats, cash, and personal property—in many cases never even charging the owner with a crime, or refusing to return property when an accused was acquitted or charges were dropped.

A 1988 *St. Petersburg Times* examination of these practices in just one county, Pinellas, in the Tampa Bay area, produced these revelations:[142]

• Following phone advice from a police dispatcher when he complained about a stray dog, Gerardo Pici put the stray in his pickup truck and dropped the dog off in the woods a mile from his home. The next day, Pinellas Park Police, who had not been available the day before to assist Pici, charged him with grand larceny of a dog, then confiscated his truck. He had to spend thousands of dollars on legal bills to get the truck back.

• Acquitted by a Clearwater jury of the felonious assault of a police officer with his BMW, William Zeig, a Tampa scientist, nevertheless lost his car through civil forfeiture.

• Even though a judge dismissed charges against Steve Steegman of theft of metal from a construction site, Pinellas Park Police continued to press forfeiture against his truck. He lost the truck, $2,000 worth of tools it contained, and thousands in legal fees after his attorney explained it would cost more than the truck was worth to fight the battle in court.

• After Benito Marerro agreed to a plea arrangement in a bad check case, he discovered the police had sold his Datsun 280Z to a salvage company in spite of the pending forfeiture case. The car had been crushed into a ball of metal scrap. The police kept the money from the sale.

But the neighboring Tampa City police were the local forfeiture champions in 1988. With an attorney, two detectives, and a secretary working full time only on forfeitures, the Tampa police confiscated over 900 motor vehicles allegedly used to commit felonies and obtained thousands of dollars in cash from their owners who were forced to buy back their own cars in "settlements" with the police—all this without any adjudication of criminal conduct, or even any charges against the owners in most cases.[143]

Police confiscation of autos for forfeiture has become a lucrative national trend. Autos are easy to seize, and valuable for quick sale unless the car title is encumbered by loans (in which case the police will usually return the car rather than mess with the paperwork and bank payoff). The police know that when they confiscate a paid-for 1990 Honda Civic with a "blue book" value of $9,050, the owner—unless he or she is very angry or very wealthy or both—is not going to spend $10,000 in legal fees, storage costs, and repairs to get the car back. In Houston, Texas, more than 4,000 cars a year are confiscated, and in New York City, over 10,000. Special police auto confiscation units have been established in Alabama, Arizona, California, New Jersey, Texas, and many other states.[144]

Before we leave the beautiful state of Florida, however, allow me to inject a note of hope regarding that fair state's forfeiture laws. Not only has the public outcry concerning the Volusia County mess caused official second thoughts (including a governor's special task force on revision of the law), the Florida Supreme Court has also had something to say on the fairness of the law. While upholding the 1980 law in principle, the court stated:

> In forfeiture proceedings the state impinges on basic constitutional rights of individuals who may never have been formally charged with any civil or criminal wrongdoing. This Court has consistently held that the [Florida] constitution requires substantial burdens of proof where state action may deprive individuals of basic rights."[145]

America under Surveillance

Earlier I mentioned the difficulties Willie Jones encountered when he paid cash for a plane ticket to Houston at the Nashville Airport, losing

$9,600 in cash to agents of the U.S. Drug Enforcement Agency (which a federal judge eventually ordered returned). Mr. Jones's problem arose from his payment in cash and his being an African-American, both factors in DEA "profiles" used to spot potential drug traffickers at public transportation hubs, especially airports. It should tell you something that the airline ticket agent-informer who turned Mr. Jones in to the DEA had already been paid thousands of dollars by the DEA for similar forfeiture candidates she had fingered at the Nashville airport.

Most Americans probably don't realize that the DEA maintains special full-time confiscation squads at major airports and pays handsome 10 percent rewards to airport employees—ticket clerks, baggage handlers, anyone who alerts them to "suspicious" people, like Mr. Jones, who turn out to have cash on them the DEA can seize. CBS television's *60 Minutes* reporters checked out these DEA airport operations in New York, Atlanta, and other cities, having a well-dressed black male undercover reporter buy a plane ticket with cash. Within minutes of every purchase, DEA agents accosted the black reporter and confiscated all his money.[146] DEA permanent surveillance operations have also been set up in designated hotels in New York, Miami, Los Angeles, and other places they consider drug activity to be common. Hotel employees are paid to report "suspicious" guests and others, including people with too much or too little luggage, guests who pay room bills in cash, or those who make multiple long-distance phone calls.[147]

Guilt by Ethnicity

At this point let me inject some very real personal concerns I have about the widespread police tactic of presuming guilt on the part of minority racial and ethnic groups in America in the context of asset forfeiture. This concern is among the principal reasons I have come to advocate forfeiture reform.

I have been struck by the fact that so many minorities are being victimized by forfeiture abuses—stopped for matching drug courier profiles of the most stereotypical kind, then having whatever cash they have on their persons seized. Those profiles may serve a valid function—to help in structuring initial searches—or they may not,[148] but they certainly shouldn't be the sole basis for the confiscation of property.

I see this police practice as devastatingly destructive. How can we as a nation continue to urge the dispossessed, the underclass, and those alienated from society to become entrepreneurs, to buy into the American Dream, to strive to climb the ladder, if their cash and property, so painfully acquired, can be so cavalierly taken away by the police? My former colleague in the House, Jack Kemp of New York, tells us that our goals in America's inner cities should be

> empowerment, ownership, and entrepreneurship.... [We should] empower individuals to take control of their lives by acquiring education, jobs, homes, private property—and by gaining access to investment capital for entrepreneurial ventures. Generations of Americans built this country by working, saving, owning a home, starting a business. This is the classic American formula for escaping poverty.[149]

Do we as a people want to tell the poor among us that social striving is useless because the rewards are apt to be confiscated by police on small pretext?

Now some might see in my concern a need to prop up our most quintessentially American of myths. I, however, see it as preventing true inequities from reinforcing distorted and destructive assumptions about American society. As social critic George Gilder writes:

> Blacks are told that the world is against them; that the prevailing powers want to keep them down; that racism and discrimination are ubiquitous except under the order and surveillance of the law; that jobs are unavailable in business; that slumlords gouge their tenants; that policemen are to be assumed guilty until proven innocent of bias and brutality; that Martin Luther King and the Kennedy brothers were killed by the white establishment.... In the United States what this image of a racist and venal country achieves ... is to incapacitate all of the poor who believe in it. Upward mobility is at least partly dependent on upward admiration: on an accurate perception of the nature of the contest and a respect for the previous winners of it. If we tell the poor that the system is corrupt, racist ... we give them a false and crippling view of society.[150]

Now, lest I give the wrong impression, I should point out that I have no great concern with protecting drug users and traffickers who happen to live in or come from poor communities. Unlike some commentators, I see no problem in throwing people out of public housing projects when convicted of drug use—provided, of course, that appropriate due process standards are met.[151] I do have the greatest concern, however, that minorities (and all American citizens) not only will lose respect for the police as a result of these lawless forfeitures but will come to view the police as enemies rather than as protectors. Jill Nelson, an African-American author and mother living in Harlem, eloquently expressed this very view recently:

> Many black and Latino people neither trust nor respect the police, much as we'd like to. Often society acts as if this attitude springs from some genetic, parental or cultural deficiency. But why would we respect them when they so often abuse their authority and so often have no respect for the people they are paid to serve and protect?[152]

I would think that those actively engaged in law enforcement would be the first to realize the validity of this concern and act to right these wrongs.

Informers' Paradise

One of the central pillars on which rests the dubious financial success of the federal forfeiture program is an army of well-paid secret informers. Forfeiture informers are paid on a contingency fee basis; the total value of the property they finger for successful forfeiture determines how much money the government pays into their personal bank accounts.

And what a great "free-enterprise" incentive this has turned out to be for the motley crew of drug pushers, ex-cons, convicts, and other social misfits who have the "qualifications" required for such grubby work. It is true that some informers are merely conscientious citizens concerned about the welfare of their nation and the future of their children—those who perhaps stumble upon some bit of information useful to the police in tracking down crooks. And some, like that airline ticket agent in Nashville, are eager and willing to be used by the police because they want the easy money.[153]

But ordinarily, informants, by their very nature, are not normal, gainfully employed, honest, upright citizens. Rather, they are or have been involved in drug or other serious criminal activity, and their motivation is to save their own skins. With criminal backgrounds and a personal stake in the outcome of a forfeiture case, paid informants have a strong incentive to lie, and they often do.

At the same time, informants are totally insulated from any problems arising from their illicit activity. If there is a forfeiture hearing, the property owner has no right to confront the informant. Thus, informants need not risk public exposure by testifying; instead, a police officer repeats what he was told by the informer. Most people never find out who accused them and their property of involvement in wrongdoing.

In 1990 and 1991, the Justice Department paid out $30 million to such informers, with a like amount budgeted for 1993. In 1992, Cary Copeland defended these expenditures as money well spent, saying, "[w]e're not paying it to them because we like them. We're paying it to them because they put money in the pot." He estimated that informers were responsible for as much as $120 million in forfeited cash flowing to federal coffers.[154] Only a few days later Jack Anderson reported in a *Washington Post* column that the highest paid federal informant in 1990 was compensated in the amount of $780,018.39, more than the salary of both the president and the vice president of the United States combined. Anderson described the high life of "a typical informant" who had worked with government agents since 1988 while dealing drugs on the side. Several times he was caught in drug deals by other police who were unaware of his federal connections, but each time the feds bailed him out because, as a DEA agent said, "[t]hey didn't want to [lose him] because he ... could get the job done.... [H]e learned how to beat the system. He had the contacts ... to smuggle large quantities of dope for us. That means [drug seizure] statistics, promotions and careers."[155]

An investigative report released by the U.S. House Committee on Government Operations in August 1992 revealed that in the prior two years the Justice Department had paid 65 informants more than $100,000 each, 24 of whom were paid between $100,000 and $250,000, and 8 received over $250,000.[156]

A Million Dollars for a Hell's Angel

Much of the federal informant program is shrouded in deep secrecy, not just to protect the identity of the informers from prospective targets of their clandestine activity but also because of the highly unsavory nature of the informers themselves. For example, Anthony Tait, a former member of the Hell's Angels motorcycle gang and an admitted drug addict, earned nearly $1 million between 1985 and 1988 as a federal informer, according to a copy of his payment schedule and his

FBI contract obtained by the *Pittsburgh Post-Gazette*. Those payments included $250,000 as a share of assets forfeited as a result of his cooperation, with payments coming from FBI offices in Anchorage and San Francisco, and from the California and federal asset forfeiture funds.[157]

The public got a rare glimpse of what goes on when Edward Vaughn testified in court that he had run a multimillion dollar international drug smuggling ring, had been a federal fugitive, and had twice served time in prison before arranging early release as a result of agreeing to work as a paid informant for the federal government. Vaughn was paid a $40,000 annual salary plus expenses by the DEA, and $500 monthly by the U.S. Marshals Service. His contract called for payment of 25 percent of all assets he caused to be forfeited to the federal government. *The Pittsburgh Post-Gazette* reported:

> [Vaughn] said he preferred arranging deals . . . known as reverse stings: the law enforcement agents pose as [drug] sellers and the targets bring cash for a buy. Those deals take cash, but not dope, off the streets. In those stings, he said, cash would be forfeited and Vaughn would get his pre-arranged quarter-share.[158]

Big-City Blunders

Boston. When police don't have a reliable informant on whom to base a "probable cause" request for a search or arrest warrant, they sometimes invent one. A 1988 investigation of the Drug Control Unit of the Boston police department revealed that its members routinely fabricated the existence of informants and lied to obtain warrants from judges. And sometime the Boston police simply get the wrong address, with mortal consequences. At 3:15 on the afternoon of March 25, 1994, a 13-member SWAT team from this same unit, wearing helmets, fatigues, and boots and armed with shotguns and 9-millimeter Glock pistols, sledgehammered through the apartment door of a 75-year-old black minister, Rev. Accelynne Williams. They were searching for guns and drugs—which they never found—based on a statement of yet another "confidential informant." At 4:00 p.m., the elderly Rev. Williams was pronounced dead of a heart attack after having been forced to the floor and handcuffed by three police officers, two holding his arms, one pinning his legs. Once he was "secure," the police noticed he was vomiting and breathing heavily and called an ambulance. The autopsy showed he died of acute myocardial infarction brought on by heart disease and "emotional stress." Six weeks and two official investigations later, the Boston police commissioner concluded the police had mistakenly raided the wrong apartment, partly because they had had a bad tip from their informant, who had been drunk the night he visited the alleged den of guns and drugs, and partly because of bad police work and lack of proper supervision and regulations governing the use of confidential informers. It was said the informant's tips were usually "considered reliable."[159] After the investigation, four officers were reassigned to other jobs and six officers had disciplinary charges lodged against them.

New York. Lying by police to support criminal charges they make is apparently common in New York City, according to a draft report of the mayor's commission investigating police corruption. After months of hearings in 1993 and 1994, the commission concluded that New York City police often make false arrests, tamper with evidence, and commit perjury on the witness stand. "Perjury is perhaps the most widespread form of police wrongdoing," the report stated, noting that the practice even has a well-known nickname among the courthouse cognoscenti—"testilying." According to New York Legal Aid Society officials, "testilying" is a common police practice that goes on without sanction by prosecutors or judges, who often cooperate by not challenging the officers' tailoring of testimony to meet constitutional objections or deficiencies in police work or reports.[160]

Cleveland. As a final example of the unquestioned "reliability" of informers, in Cleveland, Ohio, in the summer of 1992 two U.S. Postal Service inspectors arrested 19 postal workers and a local community activist, accusing all of dealing drugs, based on the undercover work of 6 informants who were allowed to pose as postal workers. When the first case went to trial in state court it immediately fell apart because the informers had faked the tape recordings of the accused dealing drugs—the voice was not even his. It turned out that the informers had bilked the Postal Service out of $250,000 in postal funds they were supposed to use in setting up drug deals and making purchases. Instead, they pocketed the money and gave the postal inspectors bags of baking soda laced with a little cocaine. Five similar Postal Service cases also came to light in other parts of the country. Most of the 19 falsely accused Ohio postal workers were dismissed, some lost their homes, several divorced, and one attempted suicide before the informer fraud was discovered.[161]

Country Snitches

Not all police departments have available the bloated resources of the federal government; in many areas local police must depend on cut-rate informants who too often prove the truth of that old adage, "you get what you pay for."

A case in point is a man whose name is Mudd—Steve R. Mudd. Starting in November 1989, Mudd was the one and only undercover agent (paid $4.65 an hour, barely minimum wage) in a marijuana investigation near Kirksville, Missouri, in rural Adair County in the northwest corner of the state. Mudd had been in drug rehabilitation, had been convicted of possession and sale of drugs, and had a history of writing bad checks. He was always broke and had no visible means of support other than odd jobs and his police pay for Operation BAD ("Bust a Dealer"). In the course of his year's "work" for the police department, Mudd gave "eyewitness information" that was used to arrest 35 people. Those arrested included Matthew Farrell, a farmer Mudd accused of cultivating and selling pot on his 60-acre farm—in an elaborate story that described night harvesting of pot with specially equipped tractors. The sheriff arrested Farrell and ordered his house and farm seized for forfeiture. A meticulous search with vacuum cleaners failed to turn up even one roach on the Farrell farm, in the house, or anywhere else. All 35 state drug cases based on Mudd's statements, including Farrell's, "went down the tubes," as county prosecutor Tom Hensley described it.[162]

But under Missouri law, proceeds from civil asset forfeitures must go directly into the state's general fund for school programs, not to the police.[163] Knowing this, prosecutor Hensley took advantage of a federal law that permits a state or local agency to convert a state seizure into a federal forfeiture.[164] When feds "adopt" the state seizure as their own, which they routinely do upon request, the state or local agency is eligible for up to 85 percent of the net proceeds from the forfeiture. And even in rural Adair County, a 60-acre farm is worth something, even if no pot is being grown there. Said Hensley, "[t]he federal sharing plan is what affected how the case was brought. . . . Seizures are kind of like bounties anyway, so why shouldn't I take it to the feds so it comes back to the local law enforcement effort?"

And what happened to Farrell and his farm? When last heard from, he and his wife were tied up in a federal forfeiture proceeding in U.S.

district court in St. Louis, notwithstanding the fact that all state criminal charges had been dismissed against him personally. County prosecutor Hensley said he didn't think Mudd had "scammed us that bad. . . . [T]here is marijuana use here and we had to get somebody. We don't get big enough cases here to get the state police here to do an investigation up right." Asked why he did not seek to have the forfeiture case dropped by federal authorities, Hensley said he was not inclined "to call down to St. Louis and tell the U.S. attorney to drop it. I've got other things to do with my time. I don't want to sound malicious but this will all work out." Assistant U.S. attorney Daniel Meuleman acknowledged that any federal case would be based on the same facts as the original state case, "[b]ut that doesn't mean we can't go ahead because there are different standards of proof involved." What Meuleman seems to be saying is, we can convict farmer Farrell on drug charges only by proving the charges "beyond a reasonable doubt"; but we can take away his farm in federal court only on the basis of mere "probable cause." Mr. Meuleman refused to say whether he would call Mudd as a witness.[165] All this gives a totally new definition to the vernacular phrase "they bought the farm."

Is it any wonder Americans are cynical about government?

Misguided Police Opposition

Police all across this nation have intimate daily knowledge of tragic events such as those I describe here. Knowing what is going on, one might think that decent and fair-minded law enforcement officials at all levels of government would be in the vanguard of those asking for reasonable reforms in civil asset forfeiture law, not just to protect innocent citizens and their property rights but to protect the police themselves from inevitable stigma under current law.

Perhaps the lure of millions of dollars for police salaries, equipment, and technical advances is too great to overcome. I sincerely hope that is not the case. But too often the police attitude is that of Sheriff Bob Vogel of Volusia County, Florida: "If you don't like the statutes . . . then you get the doggone statutes changed. We don't have to prove the fact they [property owners] are guilty."[166]

Indeed, if you listen to the police and prosecutorial rhetoric loosed in response to proposed forfeiture reform, you would think that the end of the world was at hand. Even moderate forfeiture reforms have been officially opposed by the Department of Justice, the National Association of Attorneys General, and the National District Attorneys Association. In 1991, when the Uniform Law Commission (the national conference seeking to harmonize state laws by drafting model statutes) suggested mild forfeiture reforms, all three of the above-named organizations protested by taking the unprecedented step of formally withdrawing as participants in the commission's deliberations. Instead, they presented their own "Model Asset Forfeiture Act," which contained no reforms of current law but gave government massive *new* powers to take property by forfeiture.

On the federal level, a typical negative official attitude toward forfeiture reform was arrogantly displayed by Lee J. Radek, director of the Justice Department's Asset Forfeiture Office. In an editorial in the May-June 1993 *Asset Forfeiture News*—which presumably reflected official Clinton administration policy—Radek reviewed the recent U.S. Supreme Court decisions in the *Buena Vista* and *Austin* cases,[167] acknowledging the problems these affirmations of property rights would pose for the department's forfeiture program. Apparently oblivious to the fundamental constitutional issues raised in those important cases, Radek described the decisions as "a pretty good beating from the Supreme Court," then went on to predict that Congress might adopt forfeiture reform "with dubious results probable." After lumping the Supreme Court and Congress together with "the enemies of forfeiture," all of whom delight in "kicking a good program when it's down," Radek impudently predicted he and his associates would come up with new methods of "innovative expansion" to get around the Supreme Court decisions.

So much for reasoned cooperation among the three coequal branches of the U.S. government on this important national issue.

The attitude of state-level forfeiture enforcers is not any better. Odd as it may seem, coming from the fiercely independent frontier state that gave America that rugged individualist Barry Goldwater, the Arizona legislature has adopted one of the broadest forfeiture laws in the nation. The assistant state attorney general has blatantly declared that the objective of Arizona's forfeiture law is "'social engineering' accomplished through government intercession in commercial activity harmful to the economy as a whole."[168]

Current forfeiture law allows too great a temptation for mere mortals to be able to resist. Think of it! Government officials have the power to take from private citizens their property, sell it, keep the

51

proceeds, and create for themselves an almost unlimited budget with no oversight by anyone. At the local level they can pick out items of real and personal property for their own "official" use as they please. Thus, private country clubs become police training schools and district attorneys drive new BMWs. From coast to coast, luxury acquisitions, which elected officials would never approve, abound as supplements to police budgets.

Is it any wonder that along with rape squads and murder details we now have police "forfeiture squads" out scouring the town in order to meet quotas, not for arrests and convictions but for total dollar-value confiscations? This "new math" dictates that a police officer aim at a $2 million yacht rather than at a mere $200 in the pocket of a street-level drug dealer. Besides, real criminals pose real risks. They have guns and they can be violent. Innocent property owners can't resist forfeiture unless they can afford to pay lawyers thousands of dollars—and even then the outcome is in doubt for years.

Government Vandalism

If a property owner is fortunate enough to recover his or her home, car, or boat, he or she often receives it back in a severely damaged condition. Vacant and boarded-up real property is especially subject to deterioration. And many times, as in the case of Professor Klein's yacht in Florida, government agents utterly destroy property in futile searches for contraband. It has long been the practice of U.S. Customs agents to use chain saws to rip apart imported packages or objects in a hunt for contraband. Customs found this method attractive and efficient because it never compensates anyone for the damage it inflicts. A report of the Committee on Ways and Means of the U.S. House of Representatives concluded, "[t]he U.S. Customs Service has little or no incentive to avoid damaging cargo during examinations."[169]

Untold dollars of repairs are often necessary to make the victims of forfeitures whole again, yet the federal government will not pay any damages because the Federal Tort Claims Act[170] exempts government agencies from any claims arising from the detention of "goods or merchandise" by customs or law enforcement officers. The General Accounting Office, the investigative arm of Congress, has repeatedly issued reports (nine in the last 10 years) detailing the sloppy, irresponsible way in which federal agencies allow confiscated property to be damaged, stolen, or misused.[171]

As the GAO notes, property awaiting forfeiture often devalues greatly:

> Seized conveyances devalue from aging, lack of care, inadequate storage, and other factors while awaiting forfeiture. They often deteriorate—engines freeze, batteries die, seals shrink and leak oil, boats sink, salt air and water corrode metal surfaces, barnacles accumulate on boat hulls, and windows crack from heat. On occasion, vandals steal or seriously damage conveyances.[172]

Police "Slush Funds" and Intimidation

Philadelphia city council member Joan Specter denounced the lack of executive control over police forfeiture funds, saying that "[t]he happy result for the police is that every year they get what can only be called drug slush funds. . . ." She noted that while Philadelphia police had $4 million in available forfeiture funds to spend on air-conditioning police offices, car washes, emergency postage, office supplies, and fringe benefits, the city's chemical lab, where drugs are analyzed, had a backlog of more than 3,000 cases, forcing defendants to wait months longer for trial—many in jail unable to afford bail.[173]

Law enforcement has become hooked on forfeiture as surely as the junkie nodding on the corner is hooked on drugs—the addiction of the latter has begotten the addiction of the former. They both must have their fix.

In my view, what is needed is for men and women of goodwill, certainly including responsible law enforcement officials, to come together on the issues of forfeiture law reform, to make changes that will both end the abuses and achieve the valid goal of protecting all citizens against crimes.

4. What Must Be Done

What specific steps should be taken to accomplish real reform of federal forfeiture law?

Shift the Burden of Proof

The first step is easily identifiable, a giant step for property rights, a reform every commentator and relevant interest group has recommended without exception: shift the burden of evidentiary proof in any judicial proceeding involving forfeiture.[174]

Under most federal statutory and case law, as well as the law applied in several of the states, the property owner, not the government, bears the burden of proof when he or she sues for return of confiscated property. The law reverses the normal presumption of innocence, presuming the property "guilty" unless the owner can prove otherwise. The government under current law must simply make an initial showing of "probable cause" to believe the property is "guilty" of having "facilitated" a criminal act. This is the same standard it had to meet to seize the property in the first place. Then, the burden of proof shifts to the property owner. He must show that the property is "innocent" under a preponderance of the evidence standard.

And as we have seen, "probable cause" is the weakest standard in the law—hardly an appropriate standard on which to base official confiscation of a person's property. It is probable cause that supports a search warrant authorizing nothing more than a police inspection of premises to determine if any evidence of a crime exists, well in advance of any criminal charge. Courts have defined "probable cause" as being reasonable grounds for belief in the existence of certain alleged facts—a basis for belief slightly more firm than mere suspicion. Forfeiture scholar and former Justice Department attorney David Smith correctly notes that "the government's probable cause showing serves a preliminary screening function analogous to a grand jury indictment and is no more strict 'proof' of the property's guilt than an indictment is proof of a criminal defendant's guilt."[175]

As I have mentioned, to get his property back the owner must establish that the property is "innocent," not by a standard of probable cause but by a standard of "preponderance of the evidence"—a more demanding evidentiary standard, meaning "more likely than not" that certain facts are true.[176] The probable cause standard used to seize property is far less stringent than that used in most American criminal trials (where "beyond a reasonable doubt" is the standard), and it imposes no requirement that the property owner be convicted of a crime or even indicted before the police can confiscate the property. Even a later judicial acquittal of the property owner or the dropping of charges against him does not bar or remove forfeiture.[177] Incredible as it may seem, 80 percent of those who lose property to the government through civil forfeitures are never charged with any crime.[178]

The placement of the burden of proof on the property owner in forfeiture cases dates back to the beginning of the country. When the First Congress provided forfeiture as a penalty for failure to pay customs duties it required that "the *onus probandi* shall be on the claimant."[179] This burden of proof could be characterized as no real violation of due process because in customs cases the claimant, usually a ship's captain or a commercial shipowner, either had the required documents or tax stamps in his possession or he didn't.

But with federal anti-drug and other criminal laws passed nearly two centuries later, placing the burden of proof on the owner of confiscated property has proven to be a severe and unreasonable hardship. How does an owner produce documentation or other hard evidence showing that the property was never used, and never was intended to be used, to "facilitate" the commission of a crime? This is a requirement, in effect, to prove a negative. An innocent owner faces extreme difficulty, if not impossibility, proving such a negative, while the government, as accuser, has easy access to proof of the property's use in criminal activity—if indeed such proof really does exist.

As a general principle of American law, based on fairness and practical experience, the rule is that the allocation of the burden of proof depends on which party has the more easily available means of proof. This view has been repeatedly supported by the Supreme Court in cases other than those involving forfeiture.[180]

One of the best statements of the injustice of assigning the burden of proof to the property owner appears in a dissent by U.S. District Court judge Arlen Beam:

> The current allocations of burdens and standards of proof require that the [owner] prove a negative, that the property was not used in order to facilitate illegal activity, while the government must prove almost nothing. This creates a great risk of erroneous, irreversible deprivation [of property]. . . . The allocation of burdens and standards of proof . . . is of great importance because it decides who must go forward with evidence and who bears the risk of loss should proof not rise to the standard set. In civil forfeiture cases, where owners are required to go forward with evidence and exculpate their property by a preponderance of the evidence, all risks are squarely on the owner. The government, under the current approach, need not produce any admissible evidence and may deprive citizens of property based on the rankest of hearsay and the flimsiest evidence. *This result clearly does not reflect the value of private property in our society, and makes the risk of an erroneous deprivation intolerable.*[181]

And what of the government's initial need to show probable cause? Probable cause can be established by little more than rank hearsay, gossip, or rumor.[182] Here's how it operates: one person says to another, "[t]hat guy Smith looks like he does drugs." An informant overhears this idle gossip and reports it to the police, who in turn seize Smith's residence and start forfeiture proceedings. No drugs are found and Smith is never arrested or charged with a crime. Yet Smith is forced to hire a lawyer and fight in court to get his house back—and he, and his family, may well be evicted.

You may think this sounds far-fetched, but the Justice Department has even argued in court that the probable-cause test for forfeiture can be met when a law enforcement officer simply repeats an anonymous informant's tip.[183] Of course, Justice Department lawyers are paid to put forth the policies of the administration in power, or at least the policies of those at the department who make decisions about what is to be advocated in court. In the 1980s, Justice Department lawyers repeatedly argued that hearsay evidence was adequate to support forfeiture, based on an analogy they claimed with criminal pretrial suppression hearings. In such hearings, at issue is whether certain evidence should be suppressed or admitted later at trial, usually because of the alleged illegal seizure of the evidence by the police. In such a preliminary proceeding, hearsay testimony is admitted to help a judge decide a narrow issue before trial—admissibility or suppression of evidence. It is far different in a forfeiture proceeding where hearsay evidence is allowed to decide the central issue of the proceeding—the "guilt" and forfeiture of property. Wanting to both have and eat their cake, Justice Department lawyers have always claimed that while *they* can use probable cause to seize and forfeit property, owners must meet the considerably higher "preponderance of the evidence" standard when the burden of proof shifts back to them.

Probable Cause Meets Main Street

In practical terms, what does the use of probable cause mean in the life of an owner whose property stands accused?

In Connecticut, a man named Bobby Watts was arrested for growing large quantities of marijuana on his farm. Facing a 35-year prison sentence, he was presented with a deal by federal prosecutors: turn in other pot growers and we'll go easy on you. The obliging Watts told U.S. prosecutors in New Haven that a couple named Cwiklas had 300 pounds of pot stored in their residence. (Later, Watts's story dwindled down to 200, 100, then only 1 pound of pot.) In exchange for this tale, Watts got a suspended sentence and his farm was not forfeited as it might have been. When another informant supposedly familiar with these events was asked to corroborate Watts's accusations against the Cwiklases, he failed a lie detector test on the issue.

Without any other verification of those accusations, and without searching the house first, assistant U.S. attorney Leslie Ohta filed forfeiture proceedings and confiscated the Cwiklases' residence. No pot was found and they were not charged with any crime. But the Cwiklases were forced to go into U.S. district court to try and get their home returned.[184]

There you see the practical meaning of "probable cause" supported by "hearsay" evidence. It is worth noting that assistant U.S. attorney Ohta had gained quite a public name for herself as a result of her aggressive pursuit of forfeitures, taking the homes of parents and even grandparents whose children or grandchildren used, sold, or stored pot in the homes, even though without their knowledge or consent. She insisted that such hapless relatives had a positive duty to know at all times what their offspring were doing, even in the privacy of their rooms.[185]

As fate would have it (living in glass houses division), Ms. Ohta's son was arrested for possession of marijuana and selling LSD out of her car. Court papers revealed that an undercover police agent also had bought pot from Ms. Ohta's son in his parents' home. Unlike her many forfeiture victims, Ms. Ohta was allowed by the Justice Department to keep her car and her home, but she was removed from forfeiture cases—too late to be of any help to the hapless Cwiklases, who had lost their home through the official cooperation of informant Watts and U.S. attorney Ohta.[186]

In my view, if the word still has any meaning, one might well say that it is "un-American" for our government to be able to meet its burden in court through such a flimsy standard—especially when such "probable cause" often comes from the mouths of paid criminal informants who have every reason to lie. And I say that as one who has a consistent record of support for laws that seek to curb the use of illegal drugs.

Clear and Convincing

Obviously, something has to be done to rebalance the scales of Justice and return the symbolic blindfold to her impartial eyes.

The burden of proof should stay with the government throughout the court proceedings. And the government should be forced to meet this burden by a standard of clear and convincing evidence. Clear and convincing proof is said to be the "degree of proof which will produce in mind of trier of facts a firm belief or conviction as to allegations sought to be established."[187] The government would be required to prove (1) that the unlawful act on which the forfeiture is based actually did occur and (2) that a sufficient nexus exists between the property to be seized and the alleged unlawful act. Only then should forfeiture be permitted to occur.

That is my view, but of course there are other opinions and possibilities. Standards of proof range from the minimal "probable cause" through a "preponderance of the evidence" to "clear and convincing evidence" to proof "beyond a reasonable doubt," each well-recognized evidentiary standards defined in statutory and case law.

Why not choose proof beyond a reasonable doubt? This is the standard used in criminal cases, which courts have defined as proof that would make a reasonable person "fully satisfied, entirely convinced, satisfied to a moral certainty."[188] If you can provide that sort of proof, why not bring an indictment against the owner and just throw him or her in jail, then seize his or her property through the criminal forfeiture process after conviction?[189] Well, freedom is the most precious of our rights, and against a sophisticated and well-insulated drug lord with a phalanx of high-priced attorneys, it may sometimes be impossible to build a criminal case strong enough to justify incarceration. That doesn't mean it is wrong to confiscate the alleged drug lord's property based on a lower quantum of proof. As the Supreme Court has said, "[t]he rule of evidence requiring proof beyond a reasonable doubt is generally applicable only in strictly criminal proceedings. It is founded upon the reason that a greater degree of probability should be required as a ground of judgment in criminal cases, which affect life or liberty."[190] Justice Brennan, with whom I did not always find myself in agreement, appropriately used the term "interest of transcending value"[191] to describe what is at risk for a defendant in a criminal case.

Why not "preponderance of the evidence" for a forfeiture evidence standard? Well, maybe. That is the least stringent level of proof required in most civil proceedings. It is defined as "more probable than not."[192] Once we've taken the crucial step—symbolically and practically—of switching the burden of proof, this standard will give more protection than property owners now have. In fact, those few federal civil forfeiture statutes that do put the burden of proof on the government use this standard.

But preponderance is an awfully weak standard in such a punitive environment as property forfeiture. And consider this: while civil forfeiture does serve some remedial (as opposed to punitive) goals, such as depriving "criminals of the tools by which they conduct their illegal activities,"[193] and "reimbursing the Government for investigation and enforcement expenses,"[194] there comes a point (long since passed in America) where civil penalties are so overwhelmingly punitive in nature that a high burden of proof should be assigned to the government.[195]

Thus, the standard of proof I recommend for statutory imposition on the government in such cases is "clear and convincing evidence." Incidentally, "clear and convincing" is the standard used by the state of New York in its drug forfeiture law.[196] And it is the standard the Supreme Court of Florida ruled was mandated by the Florida Constitution's due process clause.[197]

Redefine Facilitation

The "facilitation" doctrine needs some attention as well. Our drug laws subject to forfeiture all real property "which is used, or intended to be used, in any manner or part, to . . . *facilitate* the commission of" a drug crime.[198] Courts have read into this provision a requirement that there be a "substantial connection between the property and the underlying illegal transaction" to avoid forfeitures where the property "has only an incidental or fortuitous connection to criminal activity."[199] However, the connection can often be tenuous. Should a house be forfeited because a phone call setting up a drug deal was made from it and it was used as the drop-off point?[200] There is a similar provision for conveyances.[201] Courts have typically allowed forfeiture of cars used to get to the site of drug deals.[202] But what of a car that is used to get to a meeting only preliminary to a drug sale?[203] Or a car used to get to a later meeting so that a conspirator can be repaid "front money?"[204]

If civil forfeiture can be justified, it should be in relation to a defined illegal activity, a relationship that is often called the property's "nexus" to the unlawful act.[205] Forfeiture provisions usually have limiting language describing property that "facilitates" certain acts or is used "in furtherance of" unlawful activity. In my view it is important to establish a clear link between the property and the prohibited criminal activity. When civil forfeiture is used to confiscate property that has no rational relation to the crime this amounts not to civil forfeiture but to the taking of unrelated property—clearly, as punishment for the owner's criminal conduct. The danger here is one of inflicting criminal punishment without any of the normal constitutional safeguards of a criminal trial.

I have no problem with the "substantial connection" test. I would just hope that courts apply it judiciously. As forfeiture expert David Smith points out, Congress has given the courts little direction.[206] Some may be in order.

Strengthen the "Innocent-Owner" Defense

Real property used to commit or to facilitate a federal drug crime is forfeitable unless the violation was "committed or omitted without the knowledge or consent of [the] owner."[207] This qualification is of course meant to protect innocent owners. However, a number of federal courts have seriously eroded the provision's protections by ruling that the owner must have both had no knowledge of and provided no consent to the prohibited use of the property.[208] Such an interpretation would mean that property owners such as Jesse Bunch would be out of luck. Mr. Bunch owned a bar and residential apartments in a highly active drug-trafficking area in upstate New York. He did know of drug-selling activity on his premises, but took many steps to prevent it. He fired two bartenders after they were arrested at the bar for drug violations, evicted two residents following their arrests, restricted use of the rest rooms, posted signs advising patrons that they were subject to search and seizure, restricted the bar's hours of operation, and periodically called police to report drug activity in the vicinity of his property. However, drug activity continued and, notwithstanding his valiant efforts, the government seized the property.

Luckily for Mr. Bunch, although the government argued against him, an appellate court ruled that he was protected by the innocent-owner defense because of his lack of consent to the illegal drug trafficking and his reasonable—indeed heroic—efforts to end it. "Mr. Bunch, who was trying to eke out an income from a business located in a drug-infested area that posed great risks to the safety of himself and his family, . . . fulfilled his legal obligation," said the court.[209] This is only fair, and should be the proper interpretation of the innocent-owner defense, the direction in which the Supreme Court is moving in cases such as *Buena Vista Avenue*.[210]

In 1991, a similar situation confronted Gussie Mae Gantt of Montgomery, Alabama, an elderly widow. When she discovered her adult children were selling drugs out of her home she evicted them, put up "no trespassing" signs to ward off street dealers, and repeatedly called the police to report drug activity near her house. Police made no arrests, but six months later obtained a warrant and searched her house, finding no evidence of drugs. Nevertheless, a federal magistrate ordered Ms. Gantt's home seized based on police affidavits. U.S. attorney Jim Wilson, trying to justify the forfeiture, accused Ms. Gantt of complicity in drug crimes, saying, "[a]nybody that owns property can do more than [she did] to keep crack dealers from selling drugs." A U.S. district judge wasn't buying Wilson's line; he ordered her house returned, saying she "took all reasonable steps a person of her abilities could be expected to take."[211]

In some areas of the country, law enforcement authorities have revealed plans to confiscate real property on a wholesale basis as part of the war on drugs. For example, in 1992 Denver police seized three motels in a ghetto area long plagued by drug trafficking. Denver police Lt. Jerry Frazzini told the *Rocky Mountain News*, "[i]f necessary it [the seizures of property] will continue until the city owns the whole corridor."[212] That may sound at first blush a good way to combat open-air drug markets, but the implications of such a policy are horrifying. This kind of blatant drug activity occurs in older, poorer neighborhoods where property owners have little or no control over drug trafficking and most fervently wish the police did have some control. When such police "sweeps" occur, however, drug pushers move a block or two away, thus endangering even more private property as possible objects of forfeiture.

The potential for government abuse, absent a strong innocent-owner defense, is enormous, especially in conjunction with the "relation back theory" and the "taint" doctrine, which hold generally that title to real property vests in the government from the moment criminal conduct occurs within its boundaries. Such a policy enables government to take large tracts of inner-city real estate without just payment—indeed, without any compensation—surely a cruel blow to many innocent people, many of them members of the minority community. A land grab described as part of the war against drugs would be great official cover for a city that wanted to build a freeway off-ramp (or any public works) without paying land acquisition costs.

There is another disturbing aspect to the innocent-owner issue that deserves mention. It was highlighted in the forfeiture of a three-unit rental building in Englewood, California, owned by a retired Army officer and his wife. As a result of drug activity in the building, the police confiscated the apartment house. The officer, reluctant to "serve in a third war," wanted to leave law enforcement to police. The 9th Circuit U.S. Court of Appeals upheld the seizure, saying the owners were guilty of "willful dereliction of social responsibility." When asked for comment, Los Angeles police officer Carlos Lopez said, "[w]e're trying to have owners take responsibility for the people they rent to. It's part of being an owner."[213]

Admittedly there is a civic duty to report criminal conduct, but I do not believe private citizens, even if they are owners of rental properties, should be forced to do the job of the police. With no means of physical self-defense, no power of arrest, no right to search private rental units, and no immunity from civil suit based on invasion of privacy or slander, how much can a landlord reasonably be required to do? Indeed, this expanding concept of owner responsibility for tenants' activities is an easy way for government, failing in the war on drugs, to shift blame for its dereliction to private citizens.

Thus, on June 8, 1994, federal authorities seized a rundown, 22-story, 621-room hotel near Gramercy Park in New York City, based on alleged drug trafficking and violence. The building, bought in 1985 for more than $2.5 million, had been the scene of more than 122 drug-related arrests since 1991, but the U.S. attorney's office, bragging that this "represented the largest seizure in the nation," admitted that police had been unable to stem drug activity—therefore, they confiscated the building. Query: if the police cannot control crime at a particular location over a period of three years with 122 arrests, how can the building owner do what the police cannot? And why should police failure be rewarded by confiscation of this multimillion-dollar property for government benefit?[214]

A Statutory Proportionality Test

Are some forfeitures so out of line with the severity of the underlying criminal behavior that they are unconscionable—and unconstitutional?

The Supreme Court thinks so, and has now decided in the *Austin* and *Alexander* cases that forfeitures can at some point become so disproportionate that they violate the Eighth Amendment's prohibition of excessive fines.[215] It will be interesting to see how lower courts flesh out these rulings, but that does not mean Congress cannot act on the issue.

I have no problem with forfeiture that follows in the wake of defined criminal conduct, but too much of the current confiscation of property is based on technical paperwork violations and even trumped-up charges, as we have seen in numerous examples I have cited. It makes no sense for a family's home and all its worldly possessions to be taken because one family member stole UPS packages worth less than $500. Or that an innocent owner of an aircraft has to pay $16,000 in "storage fees" in order to get the government to release his jet wrongly taken based on a "technical error" in an FAA application. Or that elderly parents are thrown out of their home because a mentally unbalanced adult child grows pot in the garden.

In my mind, it is proper for Congress to conduct a thoroughgoing review of every one of the scores of forfeiture statutes, with a keen eye to limiting such punishment for minor infractions and technical mistakes. Now that the Supreme Court has instituted an Eighth Amendment proportionality test for civil forfeiture, there is every reason to attach to existing federal forfeiture provisions, wherever appropriate, a consistent statutory test on this issue. As the Eighth Circuit Court of Appeals observed when it recently urged Congress to act on the proportionality issue:

> We do not condone drug trafficking or any drug-related activities; nonetheless, we are troubled by the government's view that any property, whether it be a hobo's hovel or the Empire State Building, can be seized by the government because the owner, regardless of his or her past criminal record, engages in a single drug transaction.... [T]he government is exacting too high a penalty in relation to the offense committed....[216]

A related issue is that of "zero tolerance," a policy begun in the latter years of President Ronald Reagan's administration. The Customs Service and the U.S. Coast Guard "went overboard" in strictly enforcing forfeiture law exactly as it was written. Wherever they found even the most minute detectable amount of an illegal substance, government agents seized the ship, auto, airplane, or other conveyance. This made for lots of shock-value media publicity, but caught in this national dragnet were luxury yachts, commercial fishing ships, and research vessels, many worth millions of dollars—all because some former crew member, long since departed, had, unbeknownst to the owner, left behind a marijuana "roach" in a locker.

One of the ships seized was the Woods Hole (Massachusetts) Oceanographic Institute's *Atlantis*, done in by just such an errant sea-going roach. My House colleague from Massachusetts, Gerry Studds, denounced the seizure, telling the then Commissioner of U.S. Customs, William von Rabb, at a Capitol Hill hearing, "[i]f you can't find something better to do with your limited resources than this kind of lunacy, then maybe we've been giving you too much money."[217]

In the past, I supported the zero tolerance policy. On mature reflection, I think justice is not served through rigorous adherence to it.

The Money Problem

As former U.S. attorney general Richard Thornburgh once said, "It is truly satisfying to think that it is now possible for a drug dealer to serve time in a forfeiture-financed prison, after being arrested by agents driving a forfeiture-provided automobile, while working in a forfeiture-funded sting operation."[218]

That small satisfaction having been savored, Article I of the Constitution still gives the power of the purse—the appropriations power—to the Congress of the United States as representatives of the people.

Prior to the Comprehensive Crime Control Act of 1984, federal forfeiture revenue was deposited in the general fund of the U.S. Treasury and, as such, this money was ultimately controlled by congressional review and direction as to its intended use. Monies now collected by the Justice Department not paid to assisting state and local agencies are deposited in the Justice Department Asset Forfeiture Fund, over which Congress has little effective control.[219] That money can be used indiscriminately (and it has been) to pay for forfeiture-related expenses, to reward informants, to equip cars, boats, and planes for law enforcement purposes, to build prisons, and so forth. As I have shown in these pages, this collect-and-spend arrangement is clearly an invitation for abuse—the very agencies seizing property benefit from the proceeds. This may be less of a problem at the federal level than at the state level, where the very agent who seizes a Corvette can soon be driving it around in undercover patrols, and where small police departments can lavish high-tech gadgets on themselves. But even at the federal level, the practice is troubling. It has allowed police to view all of America as some giant national K-Mart, where prices are not just lower but nonexistent—a sort of law enforcement "pick-'n-don't-pay."

Forfeiture should be a crime-fighting weapon, not a money-making machine for law enforcement agencies. There is no reason why all funds flowing from federal forfeitures should not be subjected to annual authorization and appropriations bills passed by the Congress. This submission to the established legislative budgetary and appropriations process will provide public accountability where there is now virtually none. Of far greater importance, submitting to congressional control will curtail, if not remove, the serious distortion that diverts police anti-crime efforts into police property acquisition efforts.

Having said that, I have been around Capitol Hill long enough to know that no legislation has a realistic chance of becoming law that will take hundreds of millions—indeed, billions—of dollars away from the Justice Department and state and local police agencies—away from the war on drugs.

That is not what I propose. But the need to finance federal law enforcement can be fully met by Congress exercising its collective judgment over revenues and funding rather than leaving forfeiture-financed spending decisions to executive-level bureaucrats with a built-in conflict of interest. With a cool half billion-plus dollars in revenue annually, asset forfeiture has become one of the most glittering Christmas trees of all time; it is time for Congress to trim the ornaments and the elves. If there is a need to "take the profit out of crime"—and there surely is—there is an equally compelling need to make sure those illicit profits are used by government to fight crime.

Restrict Adoptive Forfeiture

I have previously commented in these pages on the issue of adoptive forfeiture. Under this practice, state law enforcement officers seize property under state law and bring it to a federal agency for federal forfeiture proceedings—provided that a violation of federal law has occurred and the property is forfeitable under federal law. The federal agency (DEA, FBI, Customs, etc.) then returns 85 percent of the net proceeds to the state or local agency that initiated the case. This practice is not unlike a thief shopping around to fence stolen property to the receiver who will give him the best price for his ill-gotten goods.

Why would local police authorities choose this circuitous route, thumbing their noses at state and local executive officials? For one thing, it is far more expensive and difficult for a defendant to fight a forfeiture case against all the money, might, and power of the federal executive and judicial system than that of state or local government. Often, however, federal adoption is done in order to circumvent state laws allocating funds generated by forfeiture to non-law enforcement uses. The police want to make sure they get theirs. As I have noted, in Missouri, all funds forfeited under state law go to the state's general fund, earmarked for education, none directly to the police. Federal adoption is also a means to avoid state laws that grant stronger innocent-owner defenses than are permitted under federal law and court rulings.

Legislatures in affected states rightly find this practice to be a slap in the face and a derogation of what little is left of states' rights. I don't argue with those legislators. Fund allocation formulas are political decisions that should be decided by political (meaning elected) decisionmakers. Local law enforcement has every right to lobby the executive branch for its share of the take just as any other interest group does—no more, no less. But no county prosecutor or local police chief should be given the power under federal law to override the wishes of his own state's governor or legislature, just to fatten his own office budget.

In this regard it is worth noting that the Comprehensive Crime Control Act of 1990, which was the omnibus crime bill considered by the House of Representatives in the 101st Congress, did propose that the U.S. attorney general ensure that forfeitable property not be "transferred following utilization of an adopted seizure process to circumvent any requirement of State law that limits the disposition of property forfeited to State or local agencies."[220] While this legislation did not become law, at least Congress was moving in the right direction, toward recognizing a state's right to control the disposition of its forfeiture funds.

Rep. Bill Hughes of New Jersey, my House Judiciary Committee colleague, was the original sponsor of the law allowing federal adoption of state drug cases. He now readily admits it was a mistake he would like to undo because, in his opinion, police use it as a method to play games with the system to their advantage. When he introduced legislation to repeal case adoption "it went nowhere," he said, "because law enforcement rallied and convinced everybody they needed those cuts of the pie."[221]

I believe something must be done about federal adoption—and in a manner that protects the rights of the states to control their own police and spending. A good beginning would be to require all federal agencies using forfeiture to be governed by the forfeiture laws of the states in which the property is located. When a state makes a decision regarding forfeiture policy and enacts it into law, state law enforcement agencies should not be able to conspire with federal officials to violate that state law.

I am well aware that the financial considerations involved in the present federal adoption system mean unyielding opposition from law enforcement officials at all levels to any change in the law. That should not stop Congress from trying.

Ease Post-Forfeiture Claims Procedure

Current civil forfeiture law provides a most unsatisfactory approach to resolving claims by property owners affected by a forfeiture action. If you consider yourself to be an innocent owner, you may file a proof of claim with the U.S. district court.[222] In such a case the validity of a claim will eventually be decided by a special trustee, based on applicable statutory and common law, which means many of the legal problems I have described here will confront the claimant and his or her attorney— assuming the person can afford to challenge the government at all.

To the extent that a person seeking to make a claim on the forfeited property is not an "innocent owner"—including third-party creditors or lien holders whose claims may be "innocent" but are based on financing or work or services rendered concerning the property—he may be out in the cold. Current law says such persons have no recognizable claim on the property; but they can petition the Justice Department for an equitable remedy, which Justice—without a hearing, in its sole discretion, unreviewable on its merits in court—may or may not grant as it sees fit.[223] Unlike federal bankruptcy law with two centuries of statutory and case-developed procedures, where creditors and lien-holders are allowed to participate, forfeiture claimants are left to the tender mercy of an administrative petition procedure from which there is no recourse.

Once again, this inequitable arrangement places the decision on return of the property or payment of claims in the hands of the very agency that stands to profit from its retention and denial of any and all claims. In an increasingly complex commercial world, such a Rube Goldberg system to handle claims against forfeited property invites, nay, guarantees, inequity and business disaster.

A number of specific and thoughtful suggestions for statutory changes to meet this problem of innocent third parties affected by forfeiture have been discussed and Congress should seriously consider such modifications to protect commercial and private property interests alike.[224] In my own reform legislation,[225] I propose to abolish the 10 percent bond required of those who appeal forfeitures, to provide legal counsel for the indigent claimant, to extend the claim filing time from 10 to 60 days, and to allow a claim for any damages the government may cause during its retention of the property.

5. Forfeiture Reform—Real and Proposed

In a series of cases decided in 1993, the U.S. Supreme Court at long last established important and much-needed constitutional limitations on criminal and civil forfeiture. Until then, most federal courts seemed willing to allow unlimited expansion of government forfeiture powers.[226]

There was little reason lower courts should have done otherwise. Just 20 years ago the Supreme Court itself reaffirmed the triumph of mindless government forfeiture over the rights of innocent property owners. Their holding was based solely on forfeiture's historical family tree, with little consideration of logic, equity, or the practical needs of a modern society.[227] In that 1974 case, which government attorneys subsequently cited endlessly as authority for any and every forfeiture action, a yacht-leasing company gave a charter for one of its ships for a trip from Florida to Puerto Rico. The charter document specified no illegal conduct was to occur aboard the ship. Government agents later found one marijuana cigarette, possibly left by someone who was aboard during the charter, and confiscated the ship, valued at hundreds of thousands of dollars. The Supreme Court said the leasing company had not done "all that it reasonably could to avoid having its property put to an unlawful use." If the company had, this "might" have been a constitutional defense to forfeiture. The Court never said what the company could or should have done. Perhaps go along as an uninvited nautical nanny? As justification for its decision—holding the yacht itself guilty for the pot found aboard—the Court simply recited an excellently researched history of forfeiture dating back to gored oxen and English kings' deodands. In effect, the Court said, "That's the way this legal fiction has always operated; that's the way it still works now." The *Calero-Toledo* decision became a wholesale license for law enforcement to do as it pleased with forfeitures and, worst of all, placed a ridiculous legal fiction and its associated history above the hard-won provisions of the American Bill of Rights.

The glorification and unquestioned acceptance of these ancient legal fictions have always been at the heart of the forfeiture problem.

Buena Vista Avenue and the "Taint" Doctrine

With this legal history as a backdrop, on February 24, 1993, in *United States* v. *Buena Vista Avenue, Rumson, New Jersey*,[228] the Supreme Court seriously curtailed any further expansion of one major facet of those pro-government legal fictions, known as the "relation back" doctrine. In essence, this doctrine holds that at the very moment in time at which an illegal act punishable by forfeiture occurs, that crime "taints" the property subject to forfeiture or property purchased with the proceeds of the crime and immediately "vests" in the government all right, title, and interest in the property. Magic? Well, in this quaint hypothesis we do hear a faint echo of the Crown deodand and the medieval "evil taint" cast upon an offending object, mystical incantations about which Justice Story so often spoke.[229]

Relying on the taint doctrine, the Justice Department argued in *Buena Vista* that because subsequent "owners" were blocked from receiving good title (because of the taint), they were not "innocent owners" entitled to raise that status as a defense to forfeiture.

In the case, a woman bought a house for herself and her three children with money provided by her boyfriend at the time. There was probable cause to believe that the funds were the proceeds of illegal drug trafficking. She swore she had no knowledge of their origin. The Justice Department wanted her status as an innocent-owner denied so that the house could be seized. The Court saw how inequitable the result would be: "a logical application of the Government's [position] would result in the forfeiture of property innocently acquired by persons who had been paid with illegal proceeds for providing goods or services to drug traffickers. . . ."[230] It then ruled that under common law forfeiture, the government's "title is not perfected until judicial condemnation"[231] and "[u]ntil the Government does win such a judgment . . . someone else owns the property."[232] The woman was an owner and could raise the innocent owner defense.

Austin and Proportionality

A second blow to old-time forfeiture came on June 28, 1993, in *Austin* v. *United States*,[233] an *in rem* civil proceeding in which the Court, in a rare unanimous opinion, held that civil forfeitures are subject to the Eighth Amendment, which forbids excessive fines. Richard Austin pled guilty to a South Dakota state drug charge of possessing two grams of cocaine, worth about $2,000, with intent to distribute. He received a sentence of seven years in prison. Subsequently, the federal government moved to forfeit civilly Austin's home and auto body shop, a punishment which the Court held had to be analyzed to see whether it was disproportionate to his crime.

While the Justice Department argued that only actions recognized as criminal were covered by the Eighth Amendment, the Court found that the Amendment was not limited strictly to criminal cases. It stated that "[t]he purpose of the Eighth Amendment . . . was to limit the government's power to punish. . . . 'The notion of punishment . . . cuts across the division between the civil and the criminal law.'"[234] If forfeiture served punitive, as well as remedial, purposes, it would be covered. Civil forfeiture (under the common law and as authorized by statute) clearly did serve these purposes—to punish negligent use of property, to deter people from entering the profitable drug trade. Thus, it was subject to the Eighth Amendment's excessive fine clause.

The Court did not find that the forfeiture of Austin's property was necessarily an excessive fine, nor did it set up a standard to decide this question. It simply remanded the case back to the appellate court for it to ponder. It might be years before we know what the exact parameters of the test will be.

Alexander and the Eighth Amendment

In *Alexander v. United States*,[235] a companion case handed down the same day as *Austin*, involving racketeering, obscenity, and criminal forfeiture brought under RICO, the Court decided that when the government took $9 million in business profits, 10 pieces of real estate, and 31 businesses, that sanction may have been disproportionate and excessive under the Eighth Amendment. Ferris J. Alexander had been convicted of selling copies of seven obscene magazines and videotapes at several of his stores, for which he had already been fined $100,000 and sentenced to six years in prison.

The Court rejected, 5–4, Alexander's First Amendment claims, that applying RICO's forfeiture provisions because of the sale of expressive materials would have a "chilling effect" on other merchants. As one who knows obscenity when he sees it, and opposes it, I am even more

73

disturbed by the wider implications of the government's position in the case, which are truly chilling for American freedom. Based on the government's theory, police could seize a few books or videotapes from one store operated by, say, Blockbuster Video, Brentano's, B. Dalton, Barnes & Noble, Crown Books, or any other retail chain, claim them to be "obscene," and then close down all the stores in the chain and destroy the contents of every store—all without a trial and before any judicial consideration of the merits. What does such official conduct amount to if not book burning?

In dissenting on the First Amendment issue, Justice Kennedy wrote:

> Until now I had thought one could browse through any book or film store in the United States without fear that the proprietor had chosen each item to avoid risk to the whole inventory and indeed to the business itself. This ominous, onerous threat undermines free speech and press principles essential to our personal freedom.[236]

There had been few hints the Supreme Court was moving in this new direction on forfeiture before the 1993 rulings. One came in 1989 in *United States v. Halper*,[237] in which the Court held that a civil forfeiture action following a criminal conviction in a separate proceeding—in this instance, conviction of a doctor who had overbilled the government by $585—may be so severe as to constitute not only compensation to the government for its costs but also an unconstitutional second punishment for the same offense. In a civil action the government sought to obtain $130,000 in "remedial penalties" from Dr. Halper under the False Claims Act,[238] in addition to his criminal fine of $5,000 and two-year imprisonment. The Court said such forfeiture bore no rational relationship to the goal of compensating the government for its loss, which a trial court had estimated at $16,000. The Court remanded the case to give the government the opportunity to show that its costs were higher than the trial court had estimated. If it could not do so, the civil forfeiture was barred by the double jeopardy clause of the Fifth Amendment to the Constitution.

Good and Due Process

On December 13, 1993, the Supreme Court capped a year of forfeiture reform, handing down yet another victory for property owners. In *United States v. James Daniel Good Real Property*,[239] the Court held that, absent exigent circumstances, the due process clause of the

Fifth Amendment requires that before an owner can be deprived of his real property—whether it be his home or any other real property—he is entitled to notice and a hearing. (The decision did not reach personal property, autos, cash, or bank accounts because, unlike real property, those items could be moved or concealed if the owner had notice of the government's intention to seize. With real property—effectively, land and anything nailed to the ground—the government's interests do not outweigh the property owner's due process interests in notice and a hearing.) Before the *Good* decision the government could obtain a seizure warrant based on hearsay or on a secret informer's statements and could evict the owner the same day without a hearing or without the owner's even knowing about it.

The Court wisely found that:

> The practice of ex parte seizure . . . creates an unacceptable risk of error. . . .
>
> The ex parte preseizure proceeding affords little or no protection to the innocent owner. In issuing a warrant of seizure, the magistrate judge need determine only that there is probable cause to believe that the real property was "used, or intended to be used, in any manner or part, to commit or to facilitate the commission of" a felony narcotics offense. The Government is not required to offer any evidence on the question of innocent ownership or other potential defenses a claimant might have. . . . "[F]airness can rarely be obtained by secret, one-sided determination of facts decisive of rights. . . . No better instrument has been devised for arriving at truth than to give a person in jeopardy of serious loss notice of the case against him and opportunity to meet it."[240]

Congress Must Act—Some States Have

In spite of the foregoing Supreme Court decisions, there is much remaining to be done in forfeiture reform. On the federal level, the Congress of the United States has been notably inactive on the issue of forfeiture reform, stalled by the perceived political pressures of the war on drugs. Thus far the responsibility for reform has been left to the U.S. Supreme Court, which fortunately has had the good judgment to tackle the job in the cases I have outlined.

But on the state level change is definitely happening, usually accompanied by harsh and often demagogic verbal battles between proponents and opponents. Even the New Jersey legislature, in a state with one of the broadest and most coercive forfeiture laws, is considering easing the harshest features, changing the law to require prior conviction of a crime before forfeiture, and proportionality between the criminal act and the value of the property seized.

California Leads the Way

A typical war of words raged throughout 1993 and 1994 before the California Legislature courageously reformed its forfeiture laws.

The California police forfeiture abuses, including the multimillion-dollar Los Angeles County narcotics police trials, had become a public scandal of such great moment that many legislators reversed their past support. The forfeiture law was rather severe, for example burdening the government with only a preponderance of the evidence standard of proof.[241] It is worth recalling that when Ronald Reagan was governor in 1967 he brought about repeal of the state's forfeiture law, which at that time applied only to vehicles used in drug crimes. That law had turned police into used car lot attendants and had done little to deter drug crimes. While the General Assembly passed a very progressive reform bill in 1993 to replace the sunsetting 1988 law (raising the government's standard of proof to "clear and convincing evidence"),[242] the Senate balked and nothing was passed. Many thought the pre-1988 forfeiture law—which was not particularly favorable toward the government—would automatically reemerge.[243] However, it was forgotten that that act had a sunset provision, too. For a moment, it was arguable that there was no California state forfeiture law.[244] Finally, in August 1994, compromise forfeiture reform legislation was enacted. It closely tracked pre-1988 California law. The government's standard of proof is clear and convincing evidence with respect to proceeds (if greater than $25,000) of specified criminal transactions or moneys (if greater than $25,000) furnished or intended to be furnished in exchange for a controlled substance. In all other cases—vehicles, real property, small amounts of cash—the standard is "beyond a reasonable doubt." A criminal conviction of *someone* in a related case is required before forfeiture can take place. Other reforms were included, such as a bar on a seizing agency's official use of any seized property, and a ban on law enforcement officers' or prosecutors' employment or salaries being made dependent upon their level of seizure or forfeiture.[245]

Among the more than 16,000 forfeiture cases filed in the state since 1989, the *San Jose Mercury News*,[246] in an extensive and impressive 1993 investigation, turned up numerous cases in the five counties surveyed in which property owner "victims" were never charged or convicted of any crime. Most who lost property to police seizure were not "drug lords" or "kingpins" but rather poor people who spoke little or no English—those least able to defend themselves. Interestingly, as forfeitures increased in each of the four years the old law was in effect, California drug arrests and convictions declined steadily. Confiscated illegal drugs are not worth much; property is.

Here is a sample of the Golden State record on forfeitures that prompted reform:

• After Kay Van Sant's 30-year-old son was arrested on drug-trafficking charges, the Bakersfield police went to her bank and drained her checking account of $3,912. A self-employed bookkeeper, she had not lived with her son for more than 10 years and she was never charged with any crime. She never got her money back.

• Robert De La Torres's pickup truck was seized after his cousin was arrested in it with a pound of marijuana. De La Torres, who speaks no English, tried to explain to a Kern County judge that he had loaned the truck to his cousin while he was on a trip to Mexico, but he never got a chance. Stating "the court doesn't speak Spanish," the judge awarded the truck to the police, ignoring De La Torres's pleas for an interpreter.

• Former Los Angeles narcotics detective Robert R. Sobel, who headed one of the county's most productive anti-drug squads in the 1980s, testified in court that members of his task force routinely lied under oath, falsified police reports, invented fictitious informants, planted drugs, and beat suspects to get money and valuables. Twelve L.A. County police were convicted of crimes associated with this one drug unit.

• Attorney Robin Walters, who headed the Kern County forfeiture unit for two years, saw a distinct change in that time. Police and prosecutors, he said, "have gone crazy with this law. They're rabid. They'll take anything, whether it has anything to do with drugs or not, because they know most people will never be able to get it back."

• Sacramento attorney Phil Cozens, a former prosecutor, described the discriminating attitude displayed by police when they raided a client's apartment: "They took a bottle of Lafitte Rothschild 1984, but strangely enough, they left a bottle of Dom Perignon 1982. They took some very bizarre red wines and left most champagnes and whites." In other raids police took a full set of auto tires, a child's Nintendo game, a belt buckle, and a jar of pennies.

Said California deputy attorney general Gary Schons, who helped write the original forfeiture law, "Much like a drug addict becomes addicted to drugs, law enforcement agencies have become dependent on asset forfeitures. They have to have it."

Dan Lungren, my good friend and former colleague on the House Judiciary Committee, now the attorney general of California, agreed: "We can argue about semantics, but the fact of the matter is this is the lifeblood of local law enforcement." Mr. Lungren fought for forfeiture reenactment, accusing the press of being duped by drug lords and calling the failure to reenact the law a "cease fire" in the drug war. Said Lungren:

> Unfortunately, the white powder [cocaine] bar has done a great job of getting this issue represented in the press in very distorted fashion to suggest that somehow there are wide-scale problems with this law. That is in fact, inaccurate.

On few issues do I part company with Dan Lungren, but this is one. Another of my former House colleagues, now Assemblyman John Burton of San Francisco, led the fight for forfeiture reform, saying, "[t]he way the asset forfeiture law was being applied was an assault on individual property rights and not necessarily on drug dealers. It was a significant problem." Just before an assembly vote, anonymous pamphlets were circulated in the state capitol claiming Burton was a friend of known drug dealers. In a spirited debate, Assemblyman David Knowles, a conservative Republican, summed it up: "Liberal or conservative, it's time we admit it's a dangerous thing to empower gun-toting arms of government to take away private assets without due process."[247]

Praising the General Assembly's vote for reform in 1993, the *San Jose Mercury News* commented:

> British soldiers had an annoying habit of taking things from American colonists without payment when the crown was a little short of cash. The Founding Fathers remembered vividly when they wrote the Fifth Amendment prohibition against being "deprived of life, liberty or property without due process of law."

The legislature has made Californians more "secure in their persons, papers, and effects" as the Constitution puts it [through] an unusual coalition of conservative Republicans and liberal Democrats, joined by their mistrust of police power.

The "Show Me" State Shows Us

In early 1993, at its annual session, the Missouri legislature revised its forfeiture law after the *St. Louis Post-Dispatch* and other newspapers in that state had exposed police abuses.[248] State senator Wayne Goode, a St. Louis Democrat, led the battle, introducing reform legislation in 1992 that got lost in a general revision of criminal laws that never passed. Senator Goode came back strong in 1993 and the result was a sweeping new law with significant changes: (1) for forfeiture to apply, the property owner must have been convicted of a felony "substantially related" to the forfeiture; (2) all proceeds from forfeiture go not to the police but to the state's education programs as mandated by the state constitution; and (3) police authority to employ "federal adoption" of state forfeiture cases has been severely restricted, including by requiring a prior state court hearing to determine if such case transfers should be allowed.[249]

One Kansas City observer commented:

> Missouri's state legislature is hardly on the cutting edge of innovation in criminal law reform. The success of this significant forfeiture reform demonstrates the importance of news media publicity, and the value of a persistent legislator committed on the issue.
>
> A majority of legislators simply saw the reforms as common sense. ... If such major reform can be achieved in Missouri, it can be achieved in many other states.[250]

Action in Congress

As one who has been very involved in the debate over the need for reform of our civil asset forfeiture laws, on June 15, 1993, I introduced a bill, H.R. 2417, the "Civil Asset Forfeiture Reform Act of 1993." If you needed any evidence of the broad ideological support for reform in Congress, please note that in addition to this author on the conservative right, one of my House colleagues from the liberal end of the political spectrum, Representative John Conyers of Michigan, has also been in the forefront of this reform effort. While I do not entirely agree

79

with some aspects of Mr. Conyer's approach to forfeiture reform, I salute him for being one of the first members of Congress to take a stand against the injustices being perpetrated under state and federal asset forfeiture programs.

Representative Conyer's measure, H.R. 3515, which was introduced in October 1993, goes far beyond my legislation and would essentially shut down the federal government's civil forfeiture program—a goal I know would be applauded by many.

Despite my differences with the approach of Mr. Conyers and the Congressional Black Caucus members who support his bill, we are all working in the pursuit of reform. What we need is the cooperation of the U.S. Justice Department, the U.S. Treasury Department, and all federal, state, and local law enforcement officials in enacting reform that is fair to property owners but also keeps forfeiture alive as a strong weapon in the war against crimes of all kinds. A Justice Department draft bill has been making the rounds in Washington and, while I disagree with much in it, I recognize it as a good-faith effort on the department's behalf and a good sign of things to come. It takes the vital step of switching the burden of proof, if only to a "preponderance of the evidence" standard.

I want to make clear that the legislation I introduced reflects what I consider to be a practical and possible legislative compromise, given the political realities in the U.S. Congress. I am aware my bill certainly does not go as far as many would wish, especially since I do not support abolition of all civil forfeiture. But what follows is a description of legislation that in my considered judgment has some realistic chance of becoming law.

What the Hyde Civil Asset Forfeiture Reform Act Does

1. Changes the Burden of Proof

Currently, as we have seen, it is the property owner, not the government, who is assigned the burden of proof when he sues in an attempt to get his property back. All the government need do is make an initial showing of probable cause that the property is "guilty." The property owner must then establish by a preponderance of the evidence that the property is "innocent" or otherwise not subject to forfeiture. "This probable cause standard for seizure allows the government to dispossess property owners based only upon hearsay or innuendo—'evidence' of insufficient reliability to be admissible in a court of law."[251]

The Civil Asset Forfeiture Reform Act puts the burden of proof where it belongs. The government would have to prove by clear and convincing evidence that the property is subject to forfeiture—that the unlawful act on which the forfeiture is based actually occurred and that there is a sufficient nexus between the property and the unlawful act.[252]

2. Appoints Legal Counsel for Indigents

Currently, there is no constitutional right to appointed counsel in civil forfeiture cases.[253] This is one of the reasons why so few forfeitures are challenged. Not many people can afford the thousands of dollars in legal fees required to put up a fight, and often the property is worth less than a lawyer would charge.

The Civil Asset Forfeiture Reform Act would provide legal counsel for anyone financially unable to obtain representation to challenge a federal civil forfeiture. Maximum compensation would not exceed $3,500 per attorney for representation before a U.S. district court and $2,500 per attorney for representation before an appellate court (equivalent to the maximums for appointed counsel in federal felony cases).[254] Those dollar limits could be waived in cases of "extended or complex" representation where "excess payment is necessary to provide fair compensation and the payment is approved by the chief judge of the circuit."[255] Money to pay for provision of counsel will come, appropriately enough, from the Department of Justice Assets Forfeiture Fund.

3. Protects Innocent Property Owners

Real property used to commit or to facilitate a federal drug crime is forfeitable unless the violation was "committed or omitted without the knowledge or consent of the owner."[256] This is, of course, meant to protect innocent owners. As I have discussed, however, a number of federal courts have seriously eroded the provision's protections by ruling that the owner must have both had no knowledge of *and* provided no consent to the prohibited use of the property. H.R. 2417 clarifies this confusion by stating that lack of consent and a reasonable effort to prevent illegal activity are valid defenses, by a property owner, to forfeiture.

4. Eliminates the Cost Bond Requirement

Currently, a property owner wishing to contest the seizure of property must give the court a bond in the amount of the lesser of $5,000 or 10 percent of the value of the property seized (but not less than $250).[257] This money covers court and storage costs should the government win. The cost bond requirement is unconstitutional as applied to indigent claimants[258] and serves little purpose in other cases. There is no reason why a person whose property is seized by the government should have to post a bond to defray some of the government's litigation and storage expenses in order to have the right to a day in court to contest the forfeiture. Again, one major reason why there are so few contests of forfeitures is the high cost of retaining counsel to defend a forfeiture action. The cost bond requirement is simply an additional burden on the claimant and an added deterrent to contesting the forfeiture. The Civil Asset Forfeiture Reform Act would abolish the cost bond requirement.

5. Extends the Time Period for Challenge

Currently, if a property owner wants to challenge a forfeiture, he must "file his claim within 10 days after process has been executed."[259] This time period is woefully inadequate:

> Even assuming that notice is published the next day after process is executed, the reader of the notice will have a mere nine days to file a timely claim. Most local rules require that notice be published for three successive weeks, on the assumption that interested parties will not necessarily see the first published notice. But by the time the second notice is published, more than ten days will have elapsed from the date process was executed. Thus anyone who misses the first published notice will be unable to comply with the exceedingly short time limitation for filing a claim.[260]

Even though this time limit is sometimes ignored in the interests of justice, failure to file a timely claim can result in judgment in favor of the government. The Civil Asset Forfeiture Reform Act would lengthen this period to 60 days.

6. Forces the Government to Pay for Its Negligence

Currently, the federal government is exempted from liability under the Federal Tort Claims Act for damage caused by the negligent handling or storage of property detained by law enforcement officers.[261] Property awaiting forfeiture often devalues, as I have described.

The Civil Asset Forfeiture Reform Act would simply allow property owners to sue the government for negligence.

7. Returns Property Pending Final Disposition

Currently, customs law allows for the release of property pending final disposition of a case upon payment of a full bond.[262] However, a property owner who cannot afford to secure such a bond is out of luck. Especially when the property is used in a business, its lack of availability for the time necessary to win a victory in court can force an owner into bankruptcy. Often, the property owner must settle with the government for some sum to get property back despite the government having an extremely weak case. The Civil Asset Forfeiture Reform Act specifies that property can be released if continued possession by the government would cause the claimant substantial hardship. However, conditions may be placed on release as are appropriate to preserve the availability of the property or its equivalent for forfeiture should the government eventually prevail.

The Hyde Forfeiture Reform Act and State Laws

At least 45 states have adopted their own forfeiture laws. The Civil Asset Forfeiture Reform Act would not directly affect these statutes. However, the bill would discourage the practice known as "adoptive forfeiture." As we have seen, under adoptive forfeiture, state law enforcement officers seize property under state law and, ignoring their own state and local prosecutorial officials, bring it to a federal agency for federal forfeiture that then returns 85 percent of the net proceeds to the state or local agency that initiated the case. Thus, adoptive forfeiture is often relied upon to circumvent state laws allocating forfeited assets to non-law enforcement uses.

Since the Civil Asset Forfeiture Reform Act would make the procedural going rougher for the government in federal court, many state officials would presumably decide to stick with their state courts. The result would be more money going to state- and local-level education, drug treatment, and other services funded by forfeiture under state laws. I would hope adoptive forfeiture could someday be more significantly reined in.

In Summary

Most of all, those of us engaged in this struggle need the impassioned support of an aroused American public who recognizes what is at stake in this battle—and is willing to do the difficult things necessary to persuade Congress to act.

In these pages I have tried to make clear what is at stake in the issue of civil forfeiture law: no less than the most fundamental rights American citizens have always cherished, but too often taken for granted.

Our treasured liberties are at stake in this controversy. An informed America needs to be awakened to the reality of its possible deprivation—or, should I say, forfeiture. I believe it is late, but it is not too late.

Notes

1. 18 U.S.C. sec. 1961–68 (1988 & Supp. IV 1992).

2. *United States* v. *All Assets of Statewide Auto Parts,* 971 F.2d 896 (2nd Cir. 1992); *United States* v. *$12,390,* 956 F.2d 801, 807 n.6 (8th Cir. 1992) (Beam, J., dissenting).

3. Gary Webb, "The Forfeiture Racket," *San Jose Mercury News,* reprint of articles appearing Aug.–Sept. 1993; Jeff Brazil and Steve Berry, "Tainted Cash or Easy Money?" *Orlando Sentinel,* June 14–17, 1992; Deborah Yetter, "Police Work or Piracy? The Government's Power to Take Property in Drug Cases," *Louisville Courier-Journal,* Oct. 6–7, 1991; Andrew Schneider and Mary Pat Flaherty, "Presumed Guilty: The Law's Victims in the War on Drugs," (by permission of the *Pittsburgh Post-Gazette* as originally published in the *Pittsburgh Press,* Aug. 11–Sept. 16, 1991); J. Poor and K. Rose, "Hooked on the Drug War," *St. Louis Post-Dispatch,* Apr. 28–May 5, 1991 and Oct. 6–11, 20, 1991. See also ABC Television Network, *20/20,* Apr. 2, 1993; CBS Television Network, *Street Stories,* July 9, 1992; CBS Television Network, *60 Minutes,* Apr. 5, 1992.

4. See, e.g., *Statewide Auto Parts, supra* note 2, at 905, where the court stated, "We continue to be enormously troubled by the government's increasing and virtually unchecked use of the civil forfeiture statutes and the disregard for due process that is buried in those statutes."

5. *Austin* v. *United States,* 113 S.Ct. 2801 (1993), holding that forfeitures can become so disproportionate that they may violate the Eighth Amendment prohibition against excessive fines; see chapter 5.

6. St. Thomas Aquinas, *Summa Theologica,* II–II, 66, 2, 118; Aristotle, *Politics,* Book II, c. 3.

7. James W. Ely, Jr., *The Guardian of Every Other Right* (New York: Oxford University Press, 1992).

8. T. R. Fehrenbach, *Greatness to Spare* 198 (New York: D. Van Nostrand, 1968).

9. Steven B. Duke & Albert C. Gross, "Casualties of War," *Reason,* Feb. 1994, at 22.

10. "Government Seizures Victimize Innocent," installment of Schneider & Flaherty, *supra* note 3.

11. *United States* v. *One Mercedes 560 SEL,* 919 F.2d 327, 331 (5th Cir. 1990).

12. 19 U.S.C. sec. 1615 (1988).

13. *Austin, supra* note 5; see chapter 5.

14. Dave Altimari, "Property Seized in Drug Arrests Boon to Suburbs," *New Haven Register,* May 3, 1992, at A1, A20.

15. *United States* v. *141st Street Corp.,* 911 F.2d 870 (2nd Cir. 1990).

16. "U.S. Is Returning a Third Fraternity House," *New York Times,* Sept. 15, 1991, at 26. Settlements calling for the return of the houses were later reached. The alumni association of Tau Kappa Epsilon was forced to buy back its house from the government for a "hefty sum." See Jayne Levin, "Landlords Assail House Seizures in Drug Cases," *Washington Post,* Nov. 28, 1992, at E1.

17. David B. Smith, *Prosecution and Defense of Forfeiture Cases* sec. 4.02 (New York: Matthew Bender, 1992).

18. Steven B. Duke & Albert C. Gross, *America's Longest War: Rethinking Our Tragic Crusade Against Drugs* 138 (New York: G.P. Putnam's & Sons, 1993).

19. *United States* v. *92 Buena Vista Ave.*, 113 S.Ct. 1126 (1993); see also chapter 5.

20. *United States* v. *McNamara Buick-Pontiac*, No. CV-92-2070 (E.D. N.Y. 1992); see also Steven Schwarcz & Alan Rothman, "Civil Forfeiture: A Higher Form of Commercial Law?" 62 *Fordham L. Rev.* 287 (1993) and by the same authors, "Save the Blameless from Seizure Laws," *New York Times*, Apr. 3, 1994, at F11.

21. Thomas J. Lueck, "Port Jefferson Auto Dealer Forfeits Most Assets," *New York Times*, May 20, 1992, at B1.

22. Carl Horowitz, "What Can Government Take From You?" *Investor's Business Daily*, Dec. 9, 1993, at 1, 2.

23. U.S. Department of Justice, *Annual Report of the Department of Justice Asset Forfeiture Program: 1993*, at 16.

24. Ibid.

25. Ibid., at 20.

26. U.S. Customs Service, *U.S. Customs Service Annual Report 1993*.

27. "Forfeiture Threatens Constitutional Rights," installment of Schneider & Flaherty, *supra* note 3.

28. Terrance G. Reed, *American Forfeiture Law: Property Owners Meet the Prosecutor*, Cato Institute, Policy Analysis No. 179 (Washington, D.C., 1992).

29. 18 U.S.C. secs. 981 and 1014 (1988 & Supp. IV 1992); see *United States* v. *403½ Skyline Drive, La Habra Heights, Cal.*, 797 F. Supp. 796 (C.D. Cal. 1992), forfeiting a residence because the co-owner falsely stated his place of employment on a mortgage loan application, even though all loan payments were kept current and the mortgage company suffered no harm; see also "The Pinocchio Papers," *Los Angeles Times*, July 21, 1993.

30. Stephen Koff & Carol A. Mabin, "Government Will Keep Seized Properties Going," *St. Petersburg Times*, Oct. 26, 1991, at 6B.

31. James Bovard, "Crimes of Property," *Barron's*, Aug. 9, 1993, at 10.

32. "The Health Police Are Coming" (editorial), *Wall Street Journal*, Dec. 16, 1993, at A16; see also Mark Nestmann, "Why Doctors Are Like Drug Dealers," *FEAR Chronicles*, Nov. 1992, at 9.

33. "Government Seizures Victimize Innocent," installment of Schneider & Flaherty, *supra* note 3.

34. Arthur S. Hayes, "Civil Forfeiture Laws Are Under Attack," *Wall Street Journal*, Jan. 14, 1993, at B8.

35. "House Hearings on Forfeiture Abuse Conclude," *FEAR Chronicles*, Nov. 1993, at 1, 9.

36. "Government Seizures Victimize Innocent," installment of Schneider & Flaherty, *supra* note 3.

37. "Crime Pays Big for Informants in Forfeiture Drug Cases," installment of Schneider & Flaherty, *supra* note 3. The Drug Enforcement Administration routinely

pays out 10 percent of any money seized as reward for tips such as this. In 1990, the Justice Department paid a total of $24 million to such informers.

38. *Jones* v. *U.S. Drug Enforcement Administration*, 819 F. Supp. 698, 719–21 (M.D. Tenn. 1993).

39. United Press International, "Florida Man's Plight Sparks Customs Service Bill," Mar. 13, 1992; see also J. Marston, "Customs Destroys Boat and a Dream," *St. Petersburg Times*, Feb. 5, 1993, at 8C; James Bovard, "The Custom Service's Chain Saw Massacre," *Wall Street Journal*, Mar. 27, 1992, at A14.

40. "Jet Seized, Trashed, Offered Back for $66,000," installment of Schneider & Flaherty, *supra* note 3; see also Richard Miniter, "Property Seizures on Trial," *Insight*, Feb. 22, 1993, at 10, 33.

41. "Some Who Are Acquitted Still Get Penalized," installment of Yetter, *supra* note 3.

42. Brenda Grantland, *Your House Is under Arrest: How Police Can Seize Your Home, Car, and Business Without a Trial—And How to Protect Yourself* 83–84 (Lafayette, Calif.: Financial Privacy Report Publishers, 1993). Copies may be obtained from the publishers, 251 Lafayette Circle, Suite 350, Lafayette, Calif. 94549; phone (510) 283-7051; some facts based on conversation with author.

43. *State* v. *Real Property known as 451 Rutherford Avenue*, Superior Court, Sussex County, N.J., Docket No. SSX-L-120-91; see also David A. Kaplan, "Where the Innocent Lose," *Newsweek*, Jan. 4, 1993, at 42.

44. "Urgent Fax Alert," American Preventive Health Association, P.O. Box 2111, Tacoma, Wash. 98401 (Mar. 13, 1993).

45. Tom Flook, "Feather Forfeiture: Obscure 1918 Law Used to Forfeit Feather Artwork," *FEAR Chronicles*, Dec. 1993, at 3, 9.

46. All quotations and facts regarding the Scott case are taken from *Report on the Death of Donald Scott*, Office of the District Attorney, Ventura County, Calif. (1993); see also Miniter, *supra* note 40; and by the same author, "Ill-Gotten Gains," *Reason*, Aug.–Sept., 1993, at 32–33.

47. Exodus 21:28.

48. This biblical passage is cited by nearly all legal scholars writing on forfeiture. See George C. Pratt & William B. Petersen, "Civil Forfeiture in the Second Circuit," 65 *St. John's L. Rev.* 653, 654 (1991); Jacob J. Finkelstein, "The Goring Ox: Some Historical Perspective on Deodands, Forfeitures, Wrongful Death and the Western Notion of Sovereignty," 46 *Temple L.Q.* 169 (1973).

49. The Talmud, Tractate Bab Kamma 41a.

50. "The History of Forfeiture," *Low Profile*, Dec. 1993, at 1.

51. Oliver Wendell Holmes, Jr., *The Common Law* 1–38 (1881).

52. *Calero-Toledo* v. *Pearson Yacht Leasing Co.*, 416 U.S. 663, 681 n.16 (1974).

53. "Criminal Forfeiture," 32 *Am. U.L. Rev.* 227, 233 (1982).

54. Finkelstein, *supra* note 48, at 173.

55. *Calero-Toledo*, 416 U.S., at 682.

56. Stefan B. Herpel, "Justice Forfeited, Justice Reclaimed," *Liberty*, Oct. 1993, at 19; see also Jarret B. Wollstein, "The Government's War on Property," *The Freeman*, July 1993, at 244.

57. *Calero-Toledo*, 416 U.S., at 682.

58. "The History of Forfeiture," *supra* note 50, at 1.

59. Ibid.; see also James E. Maxeiner, "Bane of American Forfeiture Law—Banished At Last?" 62 *Cornell L. Rev.* 768 (1977).

60. "The History of Forfeiture," *supra* note 50, at 1.

61. Ibid.

62. 18 U.S.C. sec. 981(b) (1988 & Supp. IV 1992), provides that "Supplemental Federal Rules for Certain Admiralty and Maritime Claims" shall govern the seizure of assets for forfeiture in U.S. district courts. Admiralty is a highly specialized area of law with a very limited number of attorneys qualified for membership in its bar, which seriously limits the right to counsel for those whose property is seized.

63. *92 Buena Vista Avenue,* 113 S.Ct., at 1131–32.

64. Fehrenbach, *supra* note 8, at 33.

65. *Legal Papers of John Adams* 106–47 (L. Wroth & H. Zubel, ed. 1965).

66. 18 U.S.C. sec. 3563 (1988 & Supp. IV 1992); see also *United States* v. *Reckmeyer,* 628 F. Supp. 616, 619 (E.D. Va. 1986).

67. *Calero-Toledo,* 416 U.S., at 683.

68. Act of July 31, 1789, secs. 12, 36, 1 Stat. 39, 47; see also Act of August 4, 1790, 1 13, 22, 27, 67, 1 Stat. 157, 161, 163, 176.

69. *The Palmyra,* 25 U.S. (12 Wheat.) 1 (1827); see also *United States* v. *1,960 Bags of Coffee,* 12 U.S. 398, 406 (1814) (Story, J., dissenting).

70. J. Piety, "Scorched Earth: How the Expansion of Civil Forfeiture Doctrine Has Laid Waste to Due Process," 45 *U. Miami L. Rev.* 911, 940 n.137 (1991); see also U.S. Department of Commerce, *Historical Statistics of the United States,* H. Doc. 33, 86th Cong., 1st Sess. 712 (1960).

71. Holmes, *supra* note 51, at 25.

72. Ibid.

73. Ibid., at 26.

74. Pratt & Petersen, *supra* note 48, at 658.

75. *Miller,* 78 U.S., at 305.

76. Ibid., at 308–10.

77. *Boyd* v. *United States,* 116 U.S. 616, 634–38 (1886).

78. "History of Forfeiture," *supra* note 50, at 2.

79. *J. W. Goldsmith, Jr.—Grant Co.* v. *United States,* 254 U.S. 505 (1921).

80. Pratt & Petersen, *supra* note 48, at 664.

81. General Accounting Office Report GAO/GGD-81-51.

82. 7 U.S.C. sec. 2156 (1988).

83. 18 U.S.C. sec. 2344 (1988).

84. 18 U.S.C. sec. 924(c) (1988 & Supp. IV 1992).

85. 18 U.S.C. sec. 1963 (1988 & Supp. IV 1992).

86. See, e.g., *State* v. *City Construction Development, Inc.,* Superior Court of Hudson County, N.J., Docket No. W-00211206-89, wherein the state seized an entire company and its assets alleging that it had bid on and obtained three contracts for which it was not eligible—even though the contracts were all performed properly!

87. 21 U.S.C. sec. 881(a) (1988 & Supp. IV 1992).

88. Psychotropic Substances Act of 1978 (found at 21 U.S.C. sec. 881(a)(6) (1988)).

89. The Comprehensive Crime Control Act of 1984 (found at 21 U.S.C. sec. 881(a)(7) (1988)).

90. 18 U.S.C. sec. 981(a)(1)(A) (1988 & Supp. IV 1992).

91. 18 U.S.C. sec. 981(a)(1)(C) (Supp. IV 1992).

92. 18 U.S.C. sec. 981(a)(1)(C) (Supp. IV 1992).

93. 18 U.S.C. sec. 981(a)(1)(F) (Supp. IV 1992).

94. 18 U.S.C. sec. 984(b)(1) (Supp. IV 1992); see also *United States* v. *All Funds Presently on Deposit or Attempted to Be Deposited in Any Accounts Maintained at American Express Bank*, 832 F. Supp. 542 (E.D. N.Y. 1993).

95. 18 U.S.C. sec. 984(b)(2) (Supp. IV 1992).

96. *Black's Law Dictionary* 650 (6th ed. 1990).

97. *United States* v. *Angiulo*, 897 F.2d 1169, 1210 (1st Cir. 1990), *cert. den.* 498 U.S. 845 (1990).

98. *United States* v. *Lizza Industries*, 775 F.2d 492, 498 (2nd Cir. 1985), *cert. den.* 475 U.S. 1082 (1986); *United States* v. *Kravitz*, 738 F.2d 102, 106 (3rd Cir. 1984).

99. Terrance Reed, "Criminal Forfeiture Under the Comprehensive Forfeiture Act of 1984: Raising the Stakes," 22 *Am. Crim. L. Rev.* 747 (1985).

100. Reed, *supra* note 28, at 18.

101. *United States* v. *Cauble*, 706 F.2d 1322, 1350 (5th Cir. 1983), *cert. den.* 456 U.S. 1005 (1984); *in accord United States* v. *Busher*, 817 F.2d 1409, 1413 (9th Cir. 1987).

102. *NOW* v. *Scheidler*, 114 S.Ct. 798 (1994).

103. *United States* v. *Porcelli*, 865 F.2d 1352, 1364 (2nd Cir. 1989) (The court remanded the case to see if the forfeiture violated the Eighth Amendment. See also chapter 5).

104. Quoted in "Perspective," *The Freeman*, July 1993, at 243.

105. "Ill-Gotten Gains," *supra* note 46, at 34.

106. 28 U.S.C. sec. 524(c)(4) (1988 & Supp. IV 1992).

107. Grantland, *supra* note 42, at 12.

108. U.S. Department of Justice, *Asset Forfeiture Fact Sheet (1993); Annual Report of the Department of Justice Asset Forfeiture Program: 1993, supra* note 23, at 15.

109. *Annual Report of the Department of Justice Asset Forfeiture Program: 1993, supra* note 23, at 16, 19.

110. Ibid., at 17.

111. Ibid., at 20.

112. *U.S. Customs Service Annual Report, supra* note 26.

113. Advertisement for auction of "seized property," *Forbes,* Jan. 31, 1994, at 18.

114. 21 U.S.C. sec. 881(d)(7) (1988), authorizes forfeiture of real property that is "used, in any manner or part, to commit, or to facilitate the commission" of any drug crime; see also *United States* v. *Approximately 50 Acres of Real Property*, 920 F.2d 900, 903 (11th Cir. 1991); *United States* v. *Parcels of Real Property*, 913 F.2d 1, 3 (1st Cir. 1990).

115. *United States* v. *Real Property & Residence*, 921 F.2d 1551, 1557 (11th Cir. 1991).

116. *United States* v. *Reynolds*, 856 F.2d 675, 676 (4th Cir. 1988).

117. "With Sketchy Data, Government Seizes House from Man's Heirs," installment of Schneider & Flaherty, *supra* note 3.

118. Bovard, *supra* note 31.

119. Tom Flook, "Police Documents Show Most Property Seizures in Michigan Resemble Curbside Shakedowns," *FEAR Chronicles*, Nov. 1993, at 3, 9.

120. "Ill-Gotten Gains," *supra* note 46, at 37.

121. Gary Webb, "Police Lobbying to Save State Asset Forfeiture Law," *San Jose Mercury News*, Sept. 7, 1993, at A1, A12.

122. *United States* v. *$12,390*, 956 F.2d, at 807 n.6.

123. Wollstein, *supra* note 56, at 249; see also *Review of Federal Asset Forfeiture Program: Hearings Before the Legislation & National Security Subcommittee of the House Committee on Government Operations*, 103rd Cong., 1st Sess. 106 (1993) (statement of Donald Carlson).

124. "Police Profit by Seizing Homes of Innocent," installment of Schneider & Flaherty, *supra* note 3.

125. Executive Office for U.S. Attorneys, Department of Justice, 38 *U.S. Attorneys Bulletin* 180 (1990).

126. Executive Office for U.S. Attorneys, Department of Justice, 37 *U.S. Attorneys Bulletin* 214 (1989).

127. "Out of Control," *Las Vegas Review Journal*, Dec. 12, 1993, at 1F, 5F.

128. 21 U.S.C. sec. 881(e) (1988).

129. John T. McQuiston, "Asset Seizure Is Questioned in Suffolk," *New York Times*, Oct. 2, 1992, at B1, B4.

130. Jon Nordheimer, "Seizure of Assets by Aggressive Drug Fighter Raises Eyebrows," *New York Times*, Aug. 2, 1992, at 37, 44, Metro section.

131. Dennis Cauchon, "Seven-Man Force Can Take Only So Much Enhancing," *USA Today*, May 18, 1992, at 7A; *Review of Federal Asset Forfeiture Program, supra* note 123, at 152.

132. Victor Merina, "Officers' Attorneys Close with a Flurry at Trial in Final Arguments of Drug Case," *Los Angeles Times*, Jan. 31, 1992, at B3.

133. Victor Merina, "Widespread Corruption in Narcotics Squad Told," *Los Angeles Times*, Mar. 19, 1992, at B3; see also Kenneth Reich & Victor Merina, "Ex-Sergeant Sentenced, Alleges Misconduct," *Los Angeles Times*, Apr. 13, 1993, at B1.

134. Reich & Merina, *supra* note 133, at B1, B8.

135. Brian Mooar & Michael York, "Three Accuse D.C. Officers of Robbery," *Washington Post*, Sept. 25, 1992, at D1; see also Gary Fields, "'Robbery With a Badge' in the Nation's Capital," *USA Today*, May 18, 1992, at 6A.

136. Wollstein, *supra* note 56, at 248.

137. Brazil & Berry, *supra* note 3.

138. "Drugs Contaminate Nearly All Money in America," installment of Schneider & Flaherty, *supra* note 3.

139. "Testimony Slams Drug Team Tactics," *Miami Herald*, Apr. 29, 1994, at B5; "Congress to Hear Testimony on Volusia Money Seizures," *St. Petersburg Times*, June 21, 1993, at 4B; Jeff Brazil, "Forfeiture Laws Seize National Scorn," *Orlando Sentinel*, Aug. 2, 1992, at A1, A21; Brazil & Berry, *supra* note 3.

140. Associated Press report, *Miami Herald*, Aug. 22, 1994, at 5B.

141. "Drug Agents More Likely to Stop Minorities," installment of Schneider & Flaherty, *supra* note 3.

142. "Seized" and other related articles, *St. Petersburg Times*, Nov. 20, 1988, at 1, 12A, 13A.

143. Ibid.

144. Jarret B. Wollstein, "How Police Confiscation Is Destroying America: Part I," *Freedom Daily*, Nov. 1993, at 20–21.

145. *Department of Law Enforcement* v. *Real Property*, 588 So.2d 957, 967 (Fla. 1991). The court also stated its concern about "the multitude of procedural deficiencies" in the law.

146. *60 Minutes*, *supra* note 3.

147. Sandra Janzen, "Informants and Undercover Investigations," *Asset Forfeiture Series*, Bureau of Justice Assistance, U.S. Department of Justice, Nov. 1990, at 21.

148. J. Finkelman, "The Second Casualty of War: Civil Liberties and the War on Drugs," 66 *U.S. Cal. L. Rev.* 1389, 1416–30 (1993).

149. Address before the National Conference of Black Mayors, Apr. 23, 1992.

150. George Gilder, *Wealth and Poverty* 99 (New York: Basic Books, 1981).

151. J. Yoskowitz, "The War on the Poor: Civil Forfeiture of Public Housing," 25 *Colum. J.L. & Soc. Prob.* 567 (1992).

152. Jill Nelson, "Blue Plague," *New York Times*, May 20, 1994, at A27.

153. At Denver's Stapleton Airport, where most drug investigations start with employees' tips, there were over 2,000 people detained by police in 1991, but only 49 arrests. One airline ticket clerk alone over a 12-month period was paid $5,834 by the U.S Treasury and Denver County. "Crime Pays Big for Informants in Forfeiture Drug Cases," installment of Schneider & Flaherty, *supra* note 3.

154. Jeff Brazil, "Informants Make Out Like Bandits," *Orlando Sentinel*, Aug. 4, 1992, at 1A.

155. Jack Anderson, "Drug Informants Beating the System," *Washington Post*, Sept. 10, 1992, at D23.

156. Brenda Grantland, *FEAR Proposal for Reform* (Sept. 30, 1992).

157. "Crime Pays Big for Informants in Forfeiture Drug Cases," installment of Schneider & Flaherty, *supra* note 3.

158. Ibid.

159. Sara Rimer, "Minister Who Sought Peace Dies in a Botched Drug Raid," *New York Times*, Mar. 28, 1994, at A1; idem, "Police Mistakes Cited in Death of Boston Man," *New York Times*, May 16, 1994, at A12.

160. "Inquiry Focuses on New York Police Practice of 'Testilying,'" *New York Times*, May 7, 1994, at 25; "Perjury by Officers Is Called Widespread," *New York Times*, Apr. 23, 1994, at 1B; Joe Sexton "False Arrest and Perjury Are Common Among New York Police," *New York Times*, Apr. 22, 1994, at A11.

161. Bill McAllister, "Con by Postal Drug Informers Puts Service in Capital Pinch," *Washington Post*, reprinted in *Miami Herald*, May 22, 1994, at 3A.

162. "35 Arrested Despite Bumbling Ways of Informant," installment of Schneider & Flaherty, *supra* note 3.

163. Mo. Ann. Stat. sec. 513.623 (Vernon 1993).

164. 19 U.S.C. sec. 1616a (1988 & Supp. IV 1992).

165. "35 Arrested Despite Bumbling Ways of Informant," installment of Schneider & Flaherty, *supra* note 3.

166. Brazil & Berry, *supra* note 3.

167. See chapter 5.

168. Cameron Holmes, "History and Purposes of Arizona Forfeiture, under A.R.S. sec. 13–4301" *American Bar Association National Institute of Forfeitures and Asset Freezes* 1 (Washington, D.C.: American Bar Association, 1990).

169. Bovard, *supra* note 39.

170. 28 U.S.C. sec. 2680(c) (1988); see also *Kosak* v. *United States*, 465 U.S. 848 (1984).

171. See "Asset Forfeiture: Need for Stronger Marshals Service Oversight of Commercial Real Property," GAO/GGD-91–82, May 1991; "Seized Conveyances, Etc.," GAO/GGD-88–30, Feb. 3, 1988; "Better Care and Disposal of Seized Cars, Etc.," GAO/PLRD-83–94, July 15, 1983.

172. "Better Care and Disposal of Seized Cars, Boats, and Planes Should Save Money and Benefit Law Enforcement," *supra* note 171, at ii.

173. Schneider & Flaherty, "Forfeiture Threatens Constitutional Rights," *supra* note 3.

174. Grantland, *supra* note 156, at 2; Reed, *supra* note 28; Stahl, "Asset Forfeiture, Burdens of Proof and the War on Drugs," 83 *J. Crim. L. & Crimin.* 274, 337 (1992); Schecter, "Fear and Loathing and the Forfeiture Laws," 75 *Cornell L. Rev.* 1151, 1182 (1990); see also National Association of Criminal Defense Lawyers, "Asset Forfeiture Fact Sheet," and American Civil Liberties Union, Draft Model Civil Forfeiture Bill.

175. Smith, *supra* note 17, at sec. 11.03.

176. 19 U.S.C. sec. 1615 (1988).

177. In *United States* v. *One Assortment of 89 Firearms*, 465 U.S. 354, 366 (1984), the Supreme Court ruled that a civil forfeiture action following a criminal acquittal does not constitute double jeopardy. Compare this with the holding in the *Halper* case discussed in chapter 5.

178. "Government Seizures Victimize Innocent," installment of Schneider & Flaherty, *supra* note 3.

179. 1 Stat. 29, 43–44 (found at 19 U.S.C. sec. 1615).

180. *United States* v. *New York, New Haven & Hartford R.R.*, 355 U.S. 253, 256 n.5 (1957); *Commercial Molasses Corp.* v. *N.Y. Tank Barge Corp.*, 314 U.S. 104, 111 (1941); see also *Wigmore on Evidence*, vol. IX, at 2486 (3rd ed. 1940).

181. *United States* v. *$12,390*, 956 F.2d at 811 (emphasis added).

182. *United States* v. *A Single Family Residence Located at 900 Rio Vista Blvd., Ft. Lauderdale*, 803 F.2d 625, 629 n.2 (11th Cir. 1986); *United States* v. *One 56-foot Motor Yacht Named "Tahuna,"* 702 F.2d 1276, 1283–84 (9th Cir. 1983).

183. See, e.g., *United States* v. *Funds in Bank Account #62538–631*, Civ. No. 89-2202-GHR (U.S.D.C. D.C.).

184. Transcript of CBS Television Network, *Street Stories*, July 9, 1992, at 14–20.

185. "Prosecutor Won't Lose Property in Son's Drug Arrest," *Hartford Courant*, Apr. 23, 1992, at A1, A3; Lynne Tuohy, "Tables May Be Turned Against Attorney," *Hartford Courant*, Mar. 22, 1992, at A1, A6.

186. Dennis Hogan, "Let Innocent People Keep Assets; Toss Out Unjust Rules," *Hartford Courant*, Mar. 25, 1992, at A2; Andre Houlding, "Feds Reorder House as Forfeitures Hit Home," *Connecticut Law Tribune*, Mar. 23, 1992, at 1, 10.

187. *Black's Law Dictionary* 227 (5th ed. 1979).

188. Ibid., at 147.

189. Criminal forfeiture requires a preexisting criminal conviction. See generally Smith, *supra* note 17, secs. 13.01–14.09. Then, the government can rely on a rebuttable presumption that property is forfeitable if it establishes by merely a preponderance of the evidence that there was no likely source for the property other than the violation. 21 U.S.C. sec. 853(d) (1988).

190. *United States v. Regan*, 232 U.S. 37, 49 (1914), quoting *Roberge v. Burnham*, 124 Mass. 277, 278 (1878).

191. *Speiser v. Randall*, 357 U.S. 513, 525 (1958).

192. *Black's Law Dictionary* 1064 (5th ed. 1979).

193. *United States v. 526 Liscum Dr., Dayton*, 866 F.2d 213, 217 (6th Cir. 1989).

194. *One Lot Emerald Cut Stones v. United States*, 409 U.S. 232, 237 (1972).

195. For an overview of the "punitive vs. remedial" issue, see Stahl, *supra* note 174, at 291–337.

196. New York CPLR sec. 1311(3) (McKinney 1985).

197. *Department of Law Enforcement v. Real Property*, 588 So.2d at 967.

198. 21 U.S.C. sec. 881(a)(7) (1988).

199. *United States v. Certain Lots in Virginia Beach*, 657 F. Supp. 1062, 1065 (E.D. Va. 1987).

200. *United States v. 124 East North Avenue*, 651 F. Supp. 1350, 1353 (N.D. Ill. 1987).

201. 21 U.S.C. sec. 881(a)(4) (1988).

202. Smith, *supra* note 17, at sec. 3.03.

203. *United States v. One 1974 Cadillac Eldorado Sedan*, 548 F.2d 421 (2nd Cir. 1977) (forfeitable).

204. *United States v. One 1972 Chevrolet Corvette*, 625 F.2d 1026 (1st Cir. 1980) (not forfeitable).

205. Smith, *supra* note 17, at sec. 3.03.

206. Ibid.

207. 21 U.S.C. sec. 881(a)(7) (1988).

208. See, e.g., *United States v. Lot 111-B, Tax Map Key 4-4-03-71(4)*, 902 F.2d 1443, 1445 (9th Cir. 1990).

209. *United States v. All Right, Title & Interest in Property Known as 710 Main St., Peekskill*, 744 F. Supp. 510 (S.D. N.Y. 1990), *aff'd on rehearing*, 753 F. Supp. 121, 125 (1990).

210. See chapter 5.

211. *United States v. One Parcel Property Located at 3855 South April St., Montgomery, Alabama*, 797 F. Supp. 933 (M.D. Ala. 1992).

212. Grantland, *supra* note 156, at 14–15.

213. Ron Galperin, "Landlords vs. Drug Dealers," *Los Angeles Times*, Jan. 12, 1992, at K1.

214. Seth Faison, "In Largest Takeover Under Narcotics Law, U.S. Seizes a Large New York City Hotel," *New York Times*, June 9, 1994, at A1, B3.

215. *Austin, supra* note 5; *Alexander v. United States*, 113 S.Ct. 2766 (1993); see chapter 5.

216. *United States v. One Parcel of Property Located at 508 Depot Street*, 964 F.2d 814, 818 (8th Cir. 1992).

217. National Association of Criminal Defense Lawyers, *Washington Digest*, July 25, 1988, at 1–2.

218. Address before Cleveland (Ohio) City Club Forum Luncheon, May 11, 1990.

219. 28 U.S.C. sec. 524(c) (1988 & Supp. IV 1992).

220. H.R. 5269, sec. 402, 101st Cong., 2d Sess. (1990).

221. "Forfeiture Threatens Constitutional Rights," installment of Schneider & Flaherty, *supra* note 3.

222. 18 U.S.C. sec. 981(b)(2) (1988 & Supp. IV 1992).

223. 28 C.F.R. secs. 9.1–.7 (1993); *United States v. A Parcel of Land in the City of Lucedale*, 791 F. Supp. 1144, 1149 (S.D. Miss. 1991).

224. See Schwarcz & Rothman, "Civil Forfeiture," *supra* note 20, at 317.

225. See chapter 5.

226. See *United States v. One Parcel of Property Located at 508 Depot St.*, 964 F.2d 814, 818 (8th Cir. 1992); *United States v. Tax Lot 1500*, 861 F.2d 232, 234 (9th Cir. 1988), *cert. den.* 110 S.Ct. 364 (1989).

227. *Calero-Toledo*, 416 U.S., at 663.

228. 113 S.Ct., at 1126.

229. *Gelston v. Hoyt*, 16 U.S. 245, 318 (1818); *United States v. 1,960 Bags of Coffee*, 12 U.S., at 406 (speaking of the "secret taint of forfeiture").

230. *Buena Vista Avenue*, 113 S.Ct., at 1135.

231. Ibid., at 1136, quoting *United States v. Stowell*, 133 U.S. 1, 16 (1889).

232. *Buena Vista Avenue*, 113 S.Ct., at 1136.

233. 113 S.Ct., at 2801.

234. Ibid., at 2805, quoting *United States v. Halper*, 490 U.S. 435, 447–48 (1989).

235. 113 S.Ct., 2766 (1993).

236. Ibid., at 2776 (Kennedy, J., dissenting).

237. 490 U.S. 435 (1989).

238. 31 U.S.C. secs. 3729–31 (1982 & Supp. V).

239. 114 S.Ct., 492 (1993).

240. Ibid., at 501–2, quoting *Joint Anti-Fascist Refugee Committee v. McGrath*, 341 U.S. 123, 170–72 (1951) (Frankfurter, J., concurring) (citations omitted).

241. California Health & Safety Code secs. 11470, 11473, 11473.2, 11473.3, 11488, 11488.4, 11488.5, 11488.6, 11489 (West 1991).

242. A.B. 114, 1993–94 Regular Session (1993).

243. Tom Daley, "Forfeiture Law Sunsets in California," *FEAR Chronicles*, Nov. 1993, at 4.

244. A.B. 114, Conference Report No. 1, Aug. 15, 1994.

245. A.B. 114 as enacted, Aug. 19, 1994.

246. Webb, *supra* note 3. Unless otherwise indicated, all facts and quotations in this chapter relating to the California forfeiture law revision are taken from these articles.

247. Quoted in Grantland, *supra* note 42, at 219.

248. See Poor & Rose, *supra* note 3.

249. Richard J. Miller, article in *FEAR Chronicles*, Nov. 1993, at 4, 5, 13; Mo. Ann. Stat. secs. 513.600–.645 (Vernon Supp. 1994).

250. Miller, *supra* note 249, at 13.

251. Reed, *supra* note 28..

252. My bill amends 19 U.S.C. sec. 1615. Most federal forfeiture statutes rely on this provision of our customs law to set the burden of proof.

253. Before *Lassiter* v. *Department of Social Services*, 452 U.S. 18 (1981), a constitutional right to appointed counsel was recognized only in cases where a litigant might lose his or her physical liberty. While *Lassiter* set up a balancing test in other situations, the Alaska Supreme Court in *Resek* v. *State*, 706 P.2d 288 (Alaska 1985), rejected the argument that counsel should be appointed in civil forfeiture cases.

254. 18 U.S.C. sec. 3006A(d)(2) (1988).

255. 18 U.S.C. sec. 3006A(d)(3) (1988).

256. 21 U.S.C. sec. 881(a)(7) (1988).

257. 19 U.S.C. sec. 1608 (1988).

258. *Wiren* v. *Eide*, 542 F.2d 757, 763–64 (9th Cir. 1976).

259. Supplemental Rule of Civil Procedure for Certain Admiralty and Maritime Claims C(6). This is the date when a U.S. court takes possession of the property through "arrest" by a federal marshal. It is *not* the date when it is initially seized by a law enforcement officer.

260. Smith, *supra* note 17, at sec. 9.03(1).

261. 28 U.S.C. sec. 2680(c) (1988).

262. 19 U.S.C. sec. 1614 (1988).

Index

About the Author

Henry Hyde, Republican of Illinois, was elected to Congress in 1974. He is a graduate of Georgetown University and of the Loyola University School of Law in Chicago. He has served as president of the Trial Lawyers Club of Chicago and as majority leader of the Illinois General Assembly. In Congress, he is a member of the Foreign Affairs Committee and has served as ranking minority member of the Civil and Constitutional Rights Subcommittee of the Judiciary Committee. He became chairman of the House Judiciary Committee in January 1995.

Cato Institute

Founded in 1977, the Cato Institute is a public policy research foundation dedicated to broadening the parameters of policy debate to allow consideration of more options that are consistent with the traditional American principles of limited government, individual liberty, and peace. To that end, the Institute strives to achieve greater involvement of the intelligent, concerned lay public in questions of policy and the proper role of government.

The Institute is named for *Cato's Letters*, libertarian pamphlets that were widely read in the American Colonies in the early 18th century and played a major role in laying the philosophical foundation for the American Revolution.

Despite the achievement of the nation's Founders, today virtually no aspect of life is free from government encroachment. A pervasive intolerance for individual rights is shown by government's arbitrary intrusions into private economic transactions and its disregard for civil liberties.

To counter that trend, the Cato Institute undertakes an extensive publications program that addresses the complete spectrum of policy issues. Books, monographs, and shorter studies are commissioned to examine the federal budget, Social Security, regulation, military spending, international trade, and myriad other issues. Major policy conferences are held throughout the year, from which papers are published thrice yearly in the *Cato Journal*. The Institute also publishes the quarterly magazine *Regulation*.

In order to maintain its independence, the Cato Institute accepts no government funding. Contributions are received from foundations, corporations, and individuals, and other revenue is generated from the sale of publications. The Institute is a nonprofit, tax-exempt, educational foundation under Section 501(c)3 of the Internal Revenue Code.

CATO INSTITUTE
1000 Massachusetts Ave., N.W.
Washington, D.C. 20001